Mutualism

Mutualism

**BUILDING THE
NEXT ECONOMY FROM
THE GROUND UP**

Sara Horowitz

with Andy Kifer

RANDOM HOUSE
NEW YORK

Published in the United States by Random House, an imprint and
division of Penguin Random House LLC, New York.

RANDOM HOUSE and the HOUSE colophon are registered trademarks
of Penguin Random House LLC.

Library of Congress Cataloging-in-Publication Data
Names: Horowitz, Sara, author. Title: Mutualism: a new social
contract for the new economy / by Sara Horowitz.
Description: New York: Random House, 2020 |
Includes bibliographical references and index.
Identifiers: LCCN 2020037289 (print) | LCCN 2020037290 (ebook) |
ISBN 9780593133521 (hardcover) | ISBN 9780593133538 (ebook)
Subjects: LCSH: Mutualism—United States. | Cooperation—
United States. | Employee fringe benefits—United States.
Classification: LCC HD3444 .H67 2020 (print) |
LCC HD3444 (ebook) | DDC 334—dc23
LC record available at https://lccn.loc.gov/2020037289

PRINTED IN CANADA ON ACID-FREE PAPER

randomhousebooks.com

2   4   6   8   9   7   5   3   1

First Edition

Illustrations by iStock/vreemous

To my great-grandmother
Sara Horowitz,
our family's matriarch who started us all on this journey

If you want to be happy, be.

—LEO TOLSTOY

Contents

Mutualism

Prologue

Mutualism is an old idea: We can look to one another to solve the most intractable problems we encounter in our lives. The instinct to help our neighbors in times of crisis is so natural to us that when we are given the tools to do so—to help our peers, and to ask for help in return—we know exactly what to do.

We need mutualism now more than ever. When the COVID-19 pandemic hit America in March 2020, we all felt an absence where our federal and local governments should have been. We were left guessing: Could we travel outside of our cities? Should we take our children out of school? Where could we get masks? We were left stranded, abandoned to our homes, afraid of running out of food. The government was like the tree we didn't know was rotten until the storm knocked it over. And for the first time, many Americans realized they had no safety net. They realized they had nowhere to turn but to each other.

So into the vacuum left by government, from New York

City to Colorado to Seattle and everywhere in between, neighbors began helping neighbors, forming mutual aid societies to meet their most urgent needs: access to food, medication, masks. An ad hoc infrastructure, powered by technologies usually reserved for corporate productivity, like Slack and Airtable, enabled donations of time, money, and even blood and plasma. Communities helped each other assemble from scratch a new, ad hoc safety net, and the process of rebuilding began. This was the mutualist instinct at its most basic and most pure.

This mutualist instinct is as old as humanity, and just as durable. It's how the earliest Americans met their most essential needs, how the labor movement transformed the American economy by building the first safety net for workers in the 1910s and '20s, how the New Deal enshrined and scaled that safety net in the middle of the American Century, and how a remarkable coalition of mutualist organizations galvanized the civil rights movement by building power over the course of decades. Throughout the years, mutualist institutions have been called many things and taken many forms—religious groups, communes, mutual aid societies, cooperatives, unions, mutuals, kibbutzim, tontines, fraternal societies, women's organizations, trade associations—but they all spring from a common impulse: If neither government nor market forces are solving a problem that you and the people in your community share, why not solve it yourself?

I've been collecting stories from our mutualist past for decades, and what I've come to see is that the most profound social changes often begin simply, when groups of people come together to solve their own problems by building the institutions they need, usually out of nothing more than basic practicality. Mutualism is really just another word for a simple truth: citizens can join together to solve their own problems, even the most intractable ones. In an era when our government has abdicated responsibility altogether, we can no longer afford to wait. And we have no choice.

I started the nonprofit that became the Freelancers Union in 1995 because freelancers, excluded from the labor legislation of the New Deal, needed a safety net. Ineligible for basic government protections, even the most successful freelancers were shouldering unbearable amounts of risk. As the ads we ran in the New York City subway in the 2000s put it: "Health Insurance vs. Paying the Rent: Welcome to Middle-Class Poverty." These freelancers had no safety net, so we built one. We were practicing mutualism, pure and simple. The Freelancers Insurance Company and brokerage we built wasn't just a successful insurance business (though with nearly $1 billion in revenue over the ten years we operated, it certainly was that); it was also a community. We listened to our members, and we built the things they asked for. We even built freelancers their own health clinic, right off Jay Street in downtown Brooklyn.

It wasn't the first time that workers have built their own safety net from scratch. I brought to the Freelancers Union a knowledge of a moment in time since lost to history, a time when the existence of this kind of mutualist safety net—built by workers, for workers—was simply the way things worked. My grandfather Israel Horowitz helped build the International Ladies' Garment Workers' Union (ILGWU), one of the most successful unions in history, from the ground up in the 1910s and '20s. This was before the New Deal, and unions like the ILGWU, whose members were on the front lines of the changing industrial economy, took their well-being into their own hands. They built for themselves insurance companies, banks, housing, and even collective summer vacation communities. Not only did their members prosper, but unions like the ILGWU also recycled the revenue from their businesses back into their communities so that their workers could experience nature, art, literature, and education—in short, so that workers could become their fullest selves.

Freelancers have been on the front lines of the disintegrating safety net for decades, but today the collapse of America's safety net affects us all. When record numbers of Americans lost their jobs—and as a result, their employer-sponsored healthcare—during the COVID-19 pandemic, the American workforce became exposed to risk to an unprecedented degree. But the collapse of the safety net was no accident: it was the result of neglect on the left and sabotage on the right, and rebuilding it isn't going to be the work of any one party. Instead, the new safety net will have to come from us. After all, mutualist cooperation is not only how Americans have built the safety net in the past; it's also how Americans have galvanized the biggest and most successful social movements in our history.

But major social change doesn't happen overnight. It begins locally, with mutualist organizations that solve specific problems for a particular community. As these local organizations become successful, typically because they find an economic model that can sustain them—dues, sales, or some other economic activity—they serve as anchors for sophisticated and sturdy mutualist ecosystems that can solve increasingly intractable problems. Over the course of decades, these mutualist ecosystems build up power—in politics and in markets—to form even broader coalitions, by building bridges with other mutualist ecosystems. Finally, with a shared goal these broad coalitions of mutualist leaders leverage their vast networks to transform society from the ground up. As mutualist organizations evolve into ecosystems and eventually into coalitions for transformation, mutualist leaders gain an ever-higher vantage point from which to see new opportunities for change. At its best, maturing mutualist activity moves through these three levels of sophistication. This is how America has remade itself again and again.

At every stage of building up the Freelancers Union, I looked for models from our past to apply to our future.

First, I first drew on the history I knew of my grandfather's ILGWU, the labor history I had learned at the Cornell University International School of Industrial and Labor Relations, and the culture of reciprocity integral to my Jewish faith. My first goal was to create a steady source of revenue for the Freelancers Union by selling affordable group health insurance to freelancers, who otherwise are left to buy insurance that costs more and covers less on the individual market. The revenues from our insurance brokerage let us steer our own ship: we could turn down funding that wasn't aligned with our goals, and the insurance we offered signaled to freelancers that our union had real value. I institutionalized the Freelancers Union by establishing a board and a network of supportive trade unionists, social sector change activists, mutualist insurance experts, tech builders and thinkers, community leaders, and supportive elected officials whom I believed in, liked, and trusted. As a result I have spent twenty-five years in conversation with workers about what they need.

Second, with a viable economic model and a strong social mission, we built an ecosystem around what freelancers needed most. My strategic North Star was the Amalgamated Clothing Workers of America, the brother organization to my family's ILGWU, and Sidney Hillman, its first president. Over time, Hillman came to see Amalgamated's mission—just like the ILGWU's—as broader than just collective bargaining. Amalgamated wanted to help its workers and their families live rich, stable, fulfilling lives. To do that, Hillman built the Amalgamated Housing Cooperative in the Bronx, the Amalgamated Life Insurance Company, the Sidney Hillman Health Clinic, and other union businesses. To fund all of it, he started his own bank: the Amalgamated Bank of New York. Hillman used the revenues from these union businesses to continue to build out the union's social mission to serve his community of workers. Astonishingly, many of these businesses still exist today. Following in Hillman's footsteps, Freelancers Union started an ecosystem of mutualist businesses of our own: on top of our insurance company and health clinic, we built a technology company to support our backend; a network of services for freelancers all over America, called Spark; and an advocacy arm that helped win protections from wage theft for freelancers through the Freelance Isn't Free Act in New York.

But I am convinced that whatever political power the Freelancers Union built over time was first and foremost thanks to the strong foundation of our economic power. When organizations for social good can fund themselves with their own independent economic mechanism, that community's political power increases dramatically. From the higher altitude afforded by that power, mutualist ecosystems can build bridges to other mutualist ecosystems to achieve change on an even wider scale.

Achieving that third and final altitude of mutualist organization—transformative social change won by broad mutualist coalitions—takes decades of dogged work. But Americans have done it before. The civil rights movement was one of the most sophisticated and effective examples in history of building bridges between mutualist ecosystems, in which two labor leaders and civil rights activists—A. Philip Randolph and Bayard Rustin—mobilized a massive mutualist constituency made up of unlikely allies, a constituency that spanned the labor movement, the civil rights movement, mutual aid societies, and Black and white religious institutions across the whole of America. Randolph and Rustin brought them all together in the March on Washington for Jobs and Freedom, which was not only a symbol of an era, but also a proof point of what mutualist thinking can achieve at scale.

To build the next safety net, we'll need to build bridges between unlikely constituencies again. But change at the massive scale we need is always anchored locally, in communities that organize themselves. To grow these mutualist organizations into mutualist ecosystems and beyond, we need to think about scaled solutions to society's problems in a new way.

Rather than big-box scale—think Amazon, Walmart, or Airbnb, which extract profit for investors rather than returning it to the communities they serve—scale through mutualism looks like a diverse but interdependent biological ecosystem. This biodiverse scale allows a common solution to a social problem to have almost infinite regional, cultural, and local variation and control. Cooperatives and unions, for example, share the same business models and goals, but they vary hugely depending on their regions and their memberships: urban or rural; skilled or unskilled; professional or low wage. Biodiversity means that scale is multifaceted and rooted in the needs of local communities, with huge numbers and a long tail.

A safety net built on a new, robust mutualist sector would show us that the problem of the social safety net doesn't need a monolithic government solution. Instead it can be a local strategy tuned toward the needs of the communities we're already a part of—a strategy that can address issues as diverse as food quality and availability, climate change, racial equity and inclusion, skills training, and housing: the elements of a strong society and a life well lived. A robust mutualist sector will help us transform our local communities back into places that solve our most essential, most human problems—into communities that put the needs of today's new workforce first.

And yet even in the wake of state and federal governments' incoherent responses to the COVID-19 pandemic, we still expect that government will always be the answer to our problems. We yearn for the solutions of our industrialized past—the New Deal and other federal safety net programs—without recognizing that, though these solutions were the right way to curb the excesses of the industrial economy, they don't apply to our future. In the middle decades of the twentieth century we needed a central and powerful government to change America: to disrupt our institutional racism, to give workers the collective power to stand up to American business, to pull us out of the Depression, and to lift the middle class. But we forget that these achievements were built on a base of organizations structured around mutualism. Mutualist organizations—especially unions, religious groups, mutual aid societies, and cooperatives—provided the leadership, the vision, the grit, and the votes that allowed disenfranchised citizens to articulate what policies they wanted to see from government. These mutualist organizations built the society they needed from the ground up, then lobbied government to protect that vision.

We need to do the same thing today. But starting in the 1970s, the left began to mistake the ends for the means. Progressives came to see government as the only tool capable of achieving social change at scale, stopped investing in organizations built around mutualist reciprocity, and, as a result, stopped replenishing the mutualist sector of our economy with new organizations capable of meeting the challenges of today's moment. We've lost our mutualist muscle memory as a society, and the result is that the mutualist sector has become not merely hollowed out—it's become almost invisible. And the social safety net—originally built on a base of mutualist organizations—is all but gone.

This book is about how we can rebuild it. If we can come to recognize and invest in the mutualist sector again, we'll see that it is perfectly positioned to deliver tomorrow's safety net. After all, when we break down the safety net into component parts—universal healthcare, education and jobs training, affordable quality food, clean drinking water, unemployment insurance, the protection of workers from exploitation—it's just a set of solutions to problems that we can begin to solve ourselves, just as we have done in the past.

We don't have to wait for government to get started, and

we shouldn't. Mutualist leaders who solve these problems locally will have the first move, and as those leaders build power through their economic independence they'll be able to petition government for the kind of regulatory changes that will let their organizations thrive. Once government begins to prefer mutualist organizations in the market, government will effectively give the mutualist sector a "job": the job of delivering safety net businesses to the communities that these mutualist organizations already serve. This will be the economic basis for the new social sector, and in the gaps left by today's government, a world of new, local organizations—organizations dedicated to providing for human needs—will flourish.

This book is divided into two parts. In the first part, I draw on hundreds of years of history to illustrate just how robust the mutualist sector of our society has always been, and how well it has helped communities in every era solve the problems they've encountered in their lives. I unpack what makes an organization mutualist, and locate where we find mutualism at work in our lives today. Then I explore what happens as mutualist organizations evolve. As mutualist leaders gain the altitude necessary to see society's problems from a higher vantage point, they build increasingly complex mutualist ecosystems that eventually achieve massive transformation through mutualist coalitions. Once you begin to recognize these patterns at work in your own life, you can begin rebuilding mutualism locally yourself.

In the second part of the book, I'll draw on our deep mutualist history to plan for our mutualist future. Today, in an era in which the structures that used to take care of us—

our government, our corporate employers—are no longer doing so, we have no choice but to build, nurture, and grow new structures so that we can take care of ourselves. I've spent the last twenty-five years organizing freelancers, the vanguard of the new economy and the new economics of work, and I've seen firsthand that the old safety net that was created to protect the industrial workforce of our past is almost gone. But a new safety net—one that addresses the reality of work as it is today—has not yet taken its place. This new safety net will need to make us secure economically, but it will also need to solve the problems of a workforce and a country that has long since evolved beyond our industrialized past.

Once we understand the power of mutualism throughout our history, I'll identify the tools we'll need to build tomorrow's mutualist safety net: the future of labor, the future of government, the future of capital, and, most important, the future of you. How can you build mutualism into your own life, or into the communities and organizations you're already a part of? If you're an elected official, a leader in an existing nonprofit, or a philanthropist, how can you work with government and business to give mutualism room to grow? We'll each need to take a look at our own lives to see where and how mutualism might already be helping us solve problems— or where it should be. Drawing on the lessons of the mutualist ecosystems of the past, we can begin to imagine what will be possible in our own communities in the future.

I started writing this book in 2018, despairing that the mutualist instinct was all but gone from American culture. It was written during a year of unprecedented change, and goes to press at a time when the outcome of that change is far from clear. A pandemic, a historic election, and a nation reckoning with its history of systemic racism in new ways—it is a year in which headlines have become irrelevant as soon as they're published.

But when I finished writing this book in the fall of 2020, I came to see that the mutualist instinct is alive and well. The explosion of mutual aid societies that let communities take care of their own during the worst days of the pandemic, the resurgence of an interest in the labor movement, the unprecedented size of the Black Lives Matter movement: at our time of greatest need, we looked to each other and we knew exactly what to do. *We* kept ourselves safe during the pandemic; *we* took to the streets to bring about the social change we wanted to see. *We* have changed the ways that we work, the ways that we earn a living, the ways that we get our most basic needs met. We've already been solving our own problems, and each of us has more agency in today's crisis than we think we do.

The next safety net is something we're going to have to build ourselves, but we've done it before. My grandfather helped do it over a century ago. But so have Americans of all colors and creeds since our nation's founding. And as we build the next safety net, we will have some advantages over those early American mutualists. For the first time in history it is possible, without even leaving your home, to use technology to find a network of hundreds of thousands of workers who wake up every day and ask themselves the same questions you ask: How do I build up my skills so I can make more money? How do I set my rates? How do I do all of this while getting my kids the best education possible? How are the rest of you getting by? Is it as hard for anyone else as it is for me? What does it mean to lead a full life with time to think, with time to be with friends and family?

What if we were able to harness today's unprecedented social interconnectivity to build an unprecedented economic interconnectivity, a long tail with millions or even billions of dollars running through new collectivized networks? What if we were able to replicate what the early unions and mutualist organizations were able to accomplish in the 1910s and '20s, but use technology to scale it to a degree that those early American innovators could never have dreamed of?

We can do this. We're doing it already. Look around you and you'll begin to see people building the necessary infrastructure: workers embedding themselves in rich networks of peers online; Zoom and other technologies that allow us to come together in groups; communities starting mutual aid circles, using technologies like Slack, Airtable, or Google Groups; technology startups conceiving of new approaches to insurance and lending; massive social change mobilized through the social networks we already belong to. We are already building the social purpose economic engines that point toward our mutualist future, a future in which we take as much responsibility for the welfare of our peers as we do for our own.

The 2010s were an era of critique, of fast capital, of snap judgments, and of quick wealth. If we are to weather the change that is coming our way, the 2020s must be an era of building, of humility, of practicality, of social change through the relentless application of our species' amazing capacity to solve problems when we need to. Future generations will measure us by the institutions we leave them. What will those institutions be?

The change we need won't start with government. It won't be foundation funded. It won't happen on Twitter. You won't vote it into office. You won't nominate it to be the candidate of a major party. People you once considered to be political allies may not understand it. MSNBC and Fox News will not know how to talk about it. Your friends may not get it.

The political realignment is producing strange bedfellows. Freelance software designers in San Francisco may realize they have more in common with factory workers in western Pennsylvania than they do with the men and women who run Apple, Facebook, or Amazon. Uber drivers in Queens may realize they're not so different from freelance writers in Los Angeles. Farmers in the reddest heartland states may realize they share an economic model with some of the bluest grocery stores in Brooklyn.

The revolution, when it comes, will start where it always has: with groups of like-minded people, yoked together by shared geography, a shared economic stake, or a shared belief, who come together to try to solve an intractable problem that government or markets either can't or won't solve for them. Profound change will come when we individually stop waiting, and collectively start building.

PART I

WHAT IS MUTUALISM?

CHAPTER 1

"Horowitz Says We Shall Make No More Brassieres"

or, A Family History of the Safety Net

When I got my first job as a lawyer in the labor movement in 1994, I assumed it would come fully loaded. Benefits just came with a job, after all, and I assumed mine would include health insurance, a retirement plan, and the protection of basic labor laws. I assumed that a safety net would be there if I needed it. I was wrong. America's safety net was already in free fall then. Today, it's almost gone entirely.

The collapse of the safety net was no accident. It was the result of neglect on the left and sabotage on the right, and it has left us with a society exposed to risk to an unprecedented degree. For many workers in the United States, the severity of this decline has become obvious only recently. But the crisis we're in today has been a long time coming.

I've been organizing freelancers for more than twenty-five years. They are the vanguard of the changing economics of work and have experienced the dissolution of the old safety net firsthand. In fact, my family had front-row seats to the rise and fall of the safety net in the twentieth century. That story—of how America's workers first built a safety net for themselves and saw government scale that safety net through the New Deal, only to see it hollowed out from within beginning in the 1970s—starts with my great-grandmother's arrival in New York around 1900. It goes like this.

I am the second Sara Horowitz in my family. The first Sara Horowitz was an immigrant, a garment worker who came to the United States from a small town on the Russian-Polish border around 1900 with her son, on the run from anti-Semites and looking for work. She settled in New York City and, like countless other new arrivals from central Europe at the time, found work in the garment district on Manhattan's West Side, which at the time was a hive of activity concentrated into a few city blocks that produced much of the clothing worn in America.

Immigrants like Sara often had worked as tailors in their home countries, designing and making whole garments—a dress, a shirt, a pair of pants—from scratch. This kind of work required skill and expertise; each garment was literally tailor-made for a single, often wealthy, client. But technology was changing, and the nature of work was changing with it. The Industrial Revolution meant that for the first time in history, it was possible to produce affordable, ready-made clothing at scale. Suddenly, more Americans than ever could afford to buy fashionable clothes for themselves, and making that clothing was too big a task for individual tailors. The era of mass-produced, low-cost clothing had arrived. So a new kind of worker—the assembly worker—was born.

My great-grandmother did piecework, making specific

parts of an item of clothing, not the whole thing. She might have sewn buttons onto dress bodices and sleeve cuffs, stooping over her detailed work for hours on end. She worked when the company needed her, but it often wasn't enough to make a decent living; she couldn't necessarily rely on having work every day. No one had thought much about what kinds of protections this new workforce might need, and the garment industry exploited that fact. Part of why business was booming in those years was that immigrant workers like Sara were cheap, and they worked hard.

But there was good news coming for workers like Sara, too. Industrial workers were starting to build organizations that helped them protect one another from exploitation by their employers, and these new unions were becoming increasingly powerful. The "needle unions" that helped protect garment workers like Sara were among the most dynamic of them all. On June 3, 1900, around the time Sara would have landed in New York, representatives from seven of these garment workers' unions met and agreed to found one of the great unions of the early labor movement: the International Ladies' Garment Workers' Union (ILGWU).

The ILGWU became a cornerstone of my family's life throughout the twentieth century. Decades later, when I was a girl, it was through the ILGWU that I first learned about the safety net and first began to develop the ideas that I now call mutualism. But the ILGWU's prominence in my family's story is largely thanks to one man: Sara Horowitz's son, Israel, my grandfather.

Israel Horowitz was only thirteen when he arrived in New York with his mother. He had always been willing to stand up for himself: according to family lore, Israel once "opened somebody's head" in the old country. (He would have been just a boy at the time, and my father used to joke that this might have had something to do with why the Horowitzes ended up in New York.) Like many new immigrants, Israel went to work as a dressmaker in the sweatshops. But he was the kind of kid who was bound to rise, and since his mother was a garment worker, the way for my grandfather to rise in the eyes of society was through his union.

Less than ten years after Sara Horowitz arrived in New York with Israel in tow, my grandfather was already making headlines. Israel was a member of the Local 25 chapter of the ILGWU, and on November 23, 1909, Local 25 executed a plan to lead a massive strike that came to be called the Uprising of the 20,000. Fifteen thousand shirtwaist makers, mostly women, walked out of factories all around New York City. Five thousand more joined the strike the following day. They were advocating for improved pay, a shorter workweek, better working conditions, and union recognition. The strike lasted for three months, until mid-February of 1910, and would be remembered as a pivotal moment in the history of the American labor movement. The ILGWU's membership ballooned: comprising roughly two thousand members at its founding in 1900, the ILGWU had won higher wages for fifteen thousand workers by the end of the strike, and Israel was part of it. According to family lore, a headline in a Bayonne, New Jersey, newspaper during the strike read:

HOROWITZ SAYS WE SHALL MAKE NO MORE BRASSIERES

My grandfather would go on to play an increasingly important role in the ILGWU. As he moved up from shop chairman to executive board member to business agent and manager of the New York Dress Board, his responsibilities gradually increased. Along the way, he met a woman named Esther, a fellow garment worker who had emigrated from Russia when she was just a girl. The two married and in 1918 had a son, Milton Horowitz, my father.

Eventually, Israel became a vice president of the union and the general manager of the union's eastern out-of-town department. As a vice president of the ILGWU, he thought about how to create a safety net for the workers. How could the union improve the lives of its members and make it easier for them to sleep at night? How could it keep their wages high and also protect them against hard times? In a changing economy in which employers weren't looking out for the well-being of their workers, how could the ILGWU become a backstop against risk?

Israel got his start during the years before the New Deal—before a national, governmentally enshrined safety net was passed into law, and people wondering how to put a roof over their heads, how to feed themselves, and how to provide for their children and their own futures had to figure it out on their own. Industrialization had created a new class of workers who could be easily exploited. Workers like Sara and Israel Horowitz had to come together to protect one another, and through organizations like the ILGWU they did.

This was a safety net built by workers, for workers. In the decades before the New Deal, there was an explosion of worker-built institutions that existed solely to meet the needs of these new industrial workers. Many of them you've probably never heard of, but some are still around today, albeit transformed, including Amalgamated Bank, which today oversees $40 billion in assets; many of New York City's original housing cooperatives, which were originally built as worker housing; and the ILGWU itself, which today lives on as part of Workers United, a union affiliated with the Service Employees International Union (SEIU).

The ILGWU wasn't just a labor union in the way we think of unions today. Yes, it collectively bargained with factory owners at the shop floor for better working conditions and wages, but its vision of the safety net extended into the very lives of its members. The lifeblood of the ILGWU was its community, workers whose commitment to one another was holistic, structural, practical, and pragmatic. While the ILGWU was busy fighting Sara Horowitz's employer for higher wages, it was simultaneously setting up local health-care clinics, housing cooperatives, retail centers, credit unions, and more. To the ILGWU, a worker like my great-grandmother wasn't just an economic unit or a piece of human capital: she was a human being, a whole person who needed to have art, nature, leisure, and education in her life.

But the money for this worker-built safety net had to come from somewhere. Unions like the ILGWU were first and foremost there to serve their members, but to do so they had to participate in markets. So while some of their members might have been self-identified socialists or communists (not uncommon among immigrants living in New York early in the twentieth century), their leaders had no choice but to become brilliantly sophisticated at building and running businesses that relied on capitalist marketplaces to provide for their members' needs. This was a period of remarkable innovation, and the ILGWU was right at the center of it— along with its counterpart, the men's clothing union, the Amalgamated Clothing Workers of America. Together, these unions represented hundreds of thousands of workers.

How were these two garment unions able to fund such a

robust, worker-built safety net? Simple: by collecting dues, which they then invested in new businesses started by the union. These businesses would not only give the unions financial security for the future but also serve their members' needs. This was not socialism (or it was a decidedly American take on socialism): these unions were using markets, not government programs, to provide for their members.

Sidney Hillman, the president of the Amalgamated Clothing Workers of America and a brilliant executive, was (to use today's argot) an agile businessman. He had his hands on the spigot of an enormous revenue stream, and when he saw a new business opportunity, he would open that spigot up. He would redirect some of his capital, hire a CEO-type leader, and suddenly have a new bank, a new housing development, or a new insurance company. As long as he thought a new venture would give him a good enough return, Hillman was eager to invest the union's money in it. Today, we might call him and David Dubinsky, who became the president of my grandfather's ILGWU in 1932, venture capitalists. But there was one major difference: Hillman and Dubinsky didn't reap profits from their startups like contemporary venture capitalists do. Instead, they recycled the profits from their experiments back into their communities to help build a better life for their workers. They weren't in it to get rich themselves.

These businesses were varied and touched every part of a worker's life. The ILGWU offered members courses in the English language, labor history, the visual and performing arts, and new trade skills. Union leaders sent mobile health units out into rural areas to give workers checkups and dental care. There was even a union-owned recreational facility in the Poconos called Unity House, where members could take their families for a modestly priced vacation and where my father worked during college.

If this sounds like a remarkably self-sufficient, well-operated community for a bunch of low-wage, working-class immigrants—well, it was. And there were dozens of other organizations just like the ILGWU. In the 1910s and '20s, the entrepreneurial period of the labor movement was in its golden age: workers could get a loan from Amalgamated Bank or medical help at the Sidney Hillman Health Center, or buy into affordable union housing in the Bronx.

With no other place to turn, working people banded together to create a self-sustaining economic and social safety net entirely for themselves. Workers were at the center of all of these organizations, and what distinguished the early unions most of all was the power of their membership. From the shop floor to the national leaders, the unions' representative structures were set up in such a way that workers had direct influence and could use that influence to get their needs met and to lead better lives. This experiment in direct democracy did not start with or come from the government. Sure, the government ostensibly represented the people, but then, as now, it was a long and arduous process to effect change only through the ballot box. With unions, by contrast, members could exercise direct control over their own lives. They paid dues, had meetings, discussed what problems they should try to solve, and voted on how to solve them.

In short, early unions provided workers with a degree of self-determination, which they used to build a tightly knit social and economic safety net—the basis of the social contract that led to the New Deal. It's not that early unions were utopias. There was infighting, prejudice, racism, and corruption, just as there is in many human institutions. But these unions, as cooperative economic mechanisms, were a direct expression of the people's will—at the time more so, I would argue, than government. Members had to work out their issues among themselves, and for a long time they did. In the process, they became skilled and robust citizens: Americans of the first order.

I never met my grandfather Israel. He died six years before I was born. But the hallmarks of the safety net he helped create—one built by workers, for workers—were all around me growing up. I remember, for instance, visiting my grandmother Esther, Israel's widow, in her comfortable if modest apartment on Manhattan's Lower East Side, in a co-op building started and run by her union. I didn't like Grandma Esther much, and these visits could feel interminable. Up until she died at age ninety-six, her English was heavily inflected with Yiddish, and she never overcame her Depression-era frugality (dessert was ice cream sprinkled with instant coffee). My sister and I didn't know what to make of her (though we came to like the dessert), but even as children, we understood that my grandmother could afford to live in this apartment only because it had been built, decades earlier, by her union.

The ILGWU's legacy was still a huge part of who we were as a family, even half a century after Israel first made headlines. I didn't think much about this then. I simply accepted it and felt comforted by it. I knew that my grandmother had an affordable home because of the ILGWU. I knew that workers like her had access to low-cost healthcare through union clinics and got loans from union banks. In the summer, Grandma Esther would take a beach chair and sit in front of the building with her friends. From a very early age, I knew that no one in my family was rich. But it seemed like everyone had enough—and I knew that this, too, was because of the ILGWU. The union's safety net was what held us all together, starting with the literal roof over my grandmother's head.

At the time, I didn't have a name for that feeling of deep-rootedness, of safety, that visiting my grandmother's apartment used to give me. It was simply the way her world worked. That concept might feel novel today, but in the earliest years of the twentieth century, it was how the new workforce—industrial workers—got their needs met. They saw problems that needed to be solved in their own lives, and they built the institutions they needed to solve them.

Today, I see that the Horowitz family's experience in the ILGWU was actually my first encounter with the economic system of mutual obligation I now call mutualism. I would later learn that it was a different frame than many brought to worker organizing, and it was a North Star that would guide me years later when I built the Freelancers Union. I can trace each of the three mutualist principles I'll explore in this book back to my experience of the ILGWU. First, the ILGWU existed to solve a social problem for a community: the whole purpose of its existence was to improve the lives of the garment workers who made up its membership. Second, it funded that social purpose with an independent economic mechanism that recycled money back into the community: dues allowed its leadership to start new worker-owned businesses like health clinics and a vacation destination that had a direct impact on the lives of the ILGWU's members.

Third, the ILGWU was built for the long term: by investing its capital in long-term bets like housing and by organizing itself with robust leadership structures (officers whose faces might change but whose roles stayed the same), the ILGWU ensured that it would continue to make a difference in its members' lives for years to come.

This lesson—that workers could build their own safety net—stuck with me. I would need it years later when I entered the workforce as a new lawyer in 1994, only to find that the safety net I'd taken for granted, the one I now needed for myself, was all but gone.

The story of that safety net—built around employer-sponsored healthcare and retirement plans, with a government backstop of Social Security, unemployment relief, and labor legislation aimed at protecting the rights and safety of workers—begins with the New Deal.

Franklin Roosevelt assumed the presidency in 1933, voted into office in the wake of the Hoover administration's failure to curb the downward spiral of the Great Depression, which began in 1929. Making good on his campaign promise of "a new deal for the American people," Roosevelt formed a two-pronged response to the crisis of the Depression. First, he scaled up government programs enormously. Whereas mutualist organizations like my grandfather's ILGWU had succeeded in improving conditions for workers in a local economy like New York City, Roosevelt needed to deploy the government's scale, power, and financial resources to effectively tackle the crisis of the Great Depression nationally. And it worked: New Deal–era reforms enshrined into law Social Security, unemployment insurance, a minimum wage, a limit on the length of the workweek, and the alphabet soup of federal agencies that provided relief to a country hit hard by the Depression. For the first time in American history, citizens could turn to their government for help.

But Roosevelt's New Deal isn't only the story of the triumph of big government. On the contrary, it's also the story of how government utilized decentralized, local institutions to build the very core of the New Deal. Roosevelt and his cabinet helped the biggest and most effective mutualist organizations of the era—unions like the ILGWU—grow and thrive. The National Labor Relations Act of 1935, also called the Wagner Act, gave these unions the right to collectively bargain for higher wages for all workers, paving the way for a decades-long period in the middle of the century during which unions mattered more than ever politically and economically, and more than a third of the American workforce was unionized.

Of course, many American workers were left out of this grand experiment in a government-scale mutualist safety net. Farmworkers and domestic workers, workforces disproportionately made up of workers of color, were not included in most labor laws. And, as I found when I entered the workforce myself, independent contractors were also excluded. For these workers, the fight to establish a safety net continues to this day.

But for much of the country, the Wagner Act put unions, and thus workers, on an equal footing with employers for the first time in history. The backstop of government support—in the form of social programs and strong labor protections—was the first pillar of the twentieth-century safety net. The second pillar—employer-sponsored benefits such as health insurance, retirement accounts, and pensions—followed soon after.

During World War II, employers faced challenges on two fronts: not only was there a labor shortage, but federally mandated wage freezes to curb wartime inflation made it harder to hire the few workers who were available. Facing a tight labor market, employers were forced to improvise. Unable to offer more money to their employees, they began to offer compensation in another form instead: "fringe benefits," usually in the form of health insurance and employer-sponsored retirement accounts. It is from this era that we get our assumptions that healthcare, insurance, and retirement savings are tied to an employer-employee relationship.

By the 1950s, fringe benefits were written into the tax code. Now employers were able to deduct the extra costs of offering such benefits from their taxable revenue. Insurance companies realized that employer-sponsored health insurance was good for their business, too. From an actuarial perspective, if every worker received the same kind of insurance (and no one had a choice in the matter), the actuarial risk pool was improved. Not only did employer-sponsored plans become the de facto way insurance companies did business, but that model also became the de facto way Americans received health insurance.

With these two pillars of the American safety net in place—employer-sponsored benefits and government protections in the form of the New Deal's reforms—risk was taken off the shoulders of American workers to an unprecedented degree. Your employer paid for your health insurance, and if something terrible happened, you received both state and private disability. Retirement savings plans helped American workers feel secure in their old age. Defined-benefit pension plans meant that some workers would be paid a predetermined number of dollars when they retired, on a predetermined date, no matter what. American workers also knew that when they retired, those savings would be bolstered by Social Security from the government.

Unions had an especially important job in the post–New Deal safety net: to keep wages high for workers through collective bargaining. Even workers who weren't unionized saw the benefits of what has been called the "union effect": the tendency of unionization to drive up wages across an industry. But collective bargaining wasn't the only reason unions were an important part of the twentieth-century safety net. Unions were also one of the primary ways American workers articulated their needs to government. The New Deal was successful in no small part because it enshrined ideas of what a safety net should look like that had originally been union innovations. Unions were the laboratories of innovation, and the government of the New Deal was just the mechanism by which those innovations could scale.

And scale they did: unions grew from representing 7.5 percent of the American workforce in 1930 to 27.1 percent in 1945. After World War II, the labor movement reached its peak in 1955, when 35 percent of American workers were unionized. Buoyed by the security of knowing that much of the risk of their day-to-day lives was being borne by the government and their employers, more Americans than ever entered a period of unprecedented prosperity.

And yet, by the early 1970s, I started to find my father wideawake in the middle of the night, unable to sleep.

I was ten, and we were both insomniacs. I'd walk into the kitchen at 1:00 a.m. to look for something to eat and find him sitting there alone, the overhead light on. Over time we developed a ritual: I'd sit down at the table in a chair facing him, and for the next twenty minutes he'd tell me stories.

This was how I learned about the heyday of the ILGWU, a world I certainly didn't learn about in my history books. I understood only some of what he was saying at the time, but later I realized he had given me a window into a lost world. Though he never worked in a sweatshop himself, he was a union-side labor lawyer who never forgot his roots as the son of two garment workers. He even taught me how to sew when I was a girl. He was born in 1918 (yes, 1918! he and my mother had me when he was older), so he remembered those years before the New Deal, waiting tables at Unity House during summers and growing up in the protective cocoon of the ILGWU in the 1920s, when the innovation machines that were the early unions were humming along smoothly.

But by my childhood, several decades into the post–New Deal economy, my father was lamenting that workers were losing the instincts and tools they needed to find and join together with their peers—tools that had enabled them to become economically and socially self-determining in the past. The strength of my father's family had always been in its social and economic interconnectedness: we were deeply rooted thanks to the ILGWU. Now my father intuitively sensed that the era in which we took care of each other was over and the era in which we took care only of ourselves was beginning.

He was right. Today, the safety net that early unions like the ILGWU built, and that the New Deal enshrined, is all but gone.

What happened?

.   .   .

It wasn't until I got a policy degree at the Kennedy School of Government at Harvard that I began to understand the story of what happened to America's safety net in the twentieth century. It's a story that touches on politics, global economics, and changing ideologies about the role of government on both sides of the political spectrum. Whole books have been written on this subject, but the short version goes something like this.

From the 1930s to the 1960s, citizens, government, policy makers, and labor leaders on the right and left alike understood that prosperity for more Americans resulted from the push-pull that existed as workers, employers, and government negotiated with one another. But by the late 1960s, both sides of the political spectrum began to shift their thinking.

On the right, thanks to economists like the Nobel laureate Milton Friedman, unions and other New Deal–era regulations came to be seen merely as obstacles to the efficient behavior of markets. The left, by contrast, came to see government as the only institution capable of solving social problems, which it did primarily in the form of major social programs like the New Deal and the Great Society: Medicare, Medicaid, an expansion of Social Security, a push to pass civil rights legislation. So while the political right cut taxes, promoted deregulation, and worked to dismantle unions directly, the left forgot that the triumph of the New Deal's reforms had in fact been two-pronged: we needed the support of strong government programs, but we also needed to nurture and grow strong, local mutualist institutions like unions that rested on an ethic of mutual obligation—that is, a keen awareness of our obligations to one another as citizens and workers.

The consequence was that Democrats, ostensibly the champions of the working class since the New Deal, began to abandon the original architects of the safety net: unions.

When I was in eleventh grade in the late 1970s, my history teacher stopped me after class and told me to read about what was happening in Youngstown, Ohio. Steelworkers were losing their jobs as plants shuttered, and despite a campaign by the United Steelworkers to preserve the Youngstown jobs, President Jimmy Carter was refusing to intervene. I started a letter-writing campaign at my school in support of the United Steelworkers, in which we urged Carter, a Democrat, to step in to help save those workers' livelihoods. It seemed clear-cut to us: the workers and their families were going to spend the next several decades in an economic tailspin, and somebody needed to do something.

Sadly, the Carter administration failed to keep the American steel industry from moving overseas. I see now that this was a foregone conclusion. By the 1970s, the predominant thinking, even among Democrats like Carter, was that markets were a force of nature, pitiless forces that had to be appeased, and if left alone, they would create a perfect capitalism and arrange American society into the winners and losers of life, the deserving and the undeserving. Business was going to go where labor was cheaper, whether America's workers liked it or not. Gone was the New Deal coalition that put workers and the labor movement at the core of the Democratic Party's agenda. Labor was now just another competing constituency, one that was becoming increasingly less relevant with every passing year.

Thomas Frank gives a succinct account of the labor movement's decline in his 2016 book, *Listen, Liberal, or What Ever Happened to the Party of the People?* Frank traces the end of the labor movement's strength to the 1968 presidential election, when the Democratic candidate, Vice President Hubert Humphrey, lost to Richard Nixon in an electoral college landslide despite the support of millions of union members. "Democratic candidates still wanted the votes of working people, of course, as well as their donations and their get-out-the-vote efforts. But between '68 and '72, unions lost their position as the premier interest group in the Democratic coalition. . . . After decades of toil on behalf of liberalism," Frank writes, unions were now taken for granted.

In their place, the Democratic Party began to court a new Ivy League–educated professional class instead. "The country had merely exchanged one elite for another; a cadre of business types for a collection of high-achieving professionals," Frank explains, arguing that Democrats and Republicans were becoming two sides of the same affluent coin. In the process, the whole notion of a society built on mutual obligation was lost. As the Oxford economist Paul Collier puts it in his 2018 book, *The Future of Capitalism: Facing the New Anxieties*, "The left and right each drifted away from their origins in the practical reciprocity of communities, and became captured by an entirely different group of people who became disproportionately influential: middle-class intellectuals."

Unions never recovered their political franchise. Forgotten by the left, many industrial and manufacturing workers—often seen as racist or parochial members of the working class—moved right. With the working class split in two, the labor movement as a whole became weaker. The ideals of reciprocal obligation that unions were built on—the idea that workers did best when they formed institutions that allowed them to help themselves—fell out of favor. By 1980,

Ronald Reagan's first campaign for president capitalized on this split, picking up the disgruntled voters abandoned by the left, the "Reagan Democrats," while the Democratic Party itself came to perform a rearguard action in the Reagan era of shrinking government and deregulated markets. Reagan was so successful at changing the rules of the game that the left had to keep whatever small pieces of progressivism it could. It reoriented itself around social programs aimed at the working poor rather than policies that gave the entire working class more agency in their own lives. This emerging neoliberal view couldn't have been more different from the one I was raised with, which saw the working class as a whole regardless of whether they were lower-wage or professional workers.

Without protection from the left, what remained of the labor movement was systematically dismantled by the right. The coup de grace came in 1981 when the Reagan administration broke a strike of thirteen thousand air traffic controllers represented by the Professional Air Traffic Controllers Organization (PATCO), who were demanding better working conditions, better pay, and a shorter workweek. When Reagan ordered all thirteen thousand back to work, only a couple thousand complied. Reagan fired the other eleven thousand, banning them from government work for the rest of their lives, and American public opinion sided with Reagan, two to one. With the breaking of PATCO, the country had completed its move to the opposite side of an ideological spectrum that had begun with Franklin Roosevelt's New Deal. "The U.S. labor movement has never recovered, and working families across the nation continue to pay the price," wrote *The Washington Post* on the twenty-fifth anniversary of the strike. "If it is true that the strike is labor's 'only true weapon,' as some unionists suggest, then practically the entire movement has been disarmed."

From 1955 to 2019, union membership declined from 35 percent of the workforce to a mere 10.3 percent, with only 6.2 percent unionized in the private sector. Since the Reagan years alone, union membership has been cut in half. Those years dealt a deathblow to labor, but they also marked a time when Americans turned away from one another and instead turned inward, toward themselves. The stock market boomed, while the wages of working men and women remained stagnant or declined; the baby boomers began to amass the capital that would make them the wealthiest generation in the history of the United States, while the middle class split into a (small) wealthy professional class and a (much larger) poorer working class.

The safety net built on mutual aid, reciprocal obligation, and solidarity that my father knew so well—that deep feeling of economic and social rootedness that had been such a part of the Horowitz family's life for a generation—was gone. The way to secure your future, suddenly, was not to turn to your neighbor and extend your hand, but rather to step over him in the rush to be on top.

It was at this moment that I, the second Sara Horowitz, entered the job market. It was the 1990s, and I was finally starting a career as a labor lawyer. I'd taken a circuitous path to get there. I studied at the Cornell University School of Industrial and Labor Relations as an undergraduate, but I wanted to understand more intimately how workers formed unions, so I became a dietary aide in a nursing home. From there (putting off what felt like the inevitable a little longer) I spent some time on a kibbutz—a kind of communal agricultural community unique to Israel, where income is pooled and divided among the group—before finally going to law school.

When I graduated, I felt like I knew the history of the labor movement and the safety net cold. Not only had my family lived that history, but I had studied it for years in college and law school. I'd helped workers organize; I'd seen how individuals in other cultures organized; I knew about the hyper-local system of mutual aid that my grandfather Israel helped build before the New Deal; I knew that the first pillar of the safety net the New Deal promised to American workers, in the form of union protections and a robust labor movement, had been unraveling for decades, especially since Reagan broke the PATCO strike.

But the problem of the disintegrating safety net was even bigger than I thought. It never occurred to me that the second pillar of the safety net—employer benefits like sick leave, vacation days, a retirement plan, and health insurance, the de facto way most workers had gotten healthcare and planned for retirement since World War II—was in the process of being dismantled as well.

So I was shocked to learn that the progressive law firm I'd just accepted a job with planned to treat me (and several of my co-workers) as an independent contractor rather than as an employee. This meant no healthcare, no 401(k), and no paid time off for vacation or illness. I was livid: not only was this illegal, but it was also an incredibly stupid thing to do to a group of labor lawyers.

What was going on?

Independent contractors, like domestic workers and farmworkers, had been excluded from the New Deal from the beginning, making it impractical for them to unionize and leaving them out of the American safety net altogether. This hadn't been an issue when most workers were employees. But now that was changing.

This was 1994, and with every passing year employers relied more and more on temporary workers—freelancers, temps, and contract employees—to do work that had for years been done by full-fledged employees. Employers preferred working with independent contractors for certain kinds of quick, temporary, or focused jobs. Not only was hiring an independent contractor more flexible than hiring a full-time employee, but it was cheaper, too. Independent contractors could do the same work once done by employees, but an employer was under no obligation to pay for their healthcare, contribute to their retirement account, or retain them if the company's needs changed. I was living through the collapse of the second pillar of the American safety net: employer-sponsored benefits.

What could I do? I started by talking with my friends and colleagues at the firm. We didn't do much besides gripe—at first. But it wasn't long before our frustration began to crystallize into something clearer in my head. If America's workers could no longer rely on the protection of either their government or their employers in periods of crisis, what was left of the twentieth-century safety net? If both these pillars were gone, to whom could we turn when disaster struck?

The answer, I realized, was rooted in what I'd first learned about the safety net when I was a girl visiting my grandmother Esther or listening to my father tell me stories about my grandfather Israel and the ILGWU at the kitchen table when I couldn't sleep. The next safety net, I realized, would have to be built by us—by workers, for workers—based on reciprocity, shared risk, and a strong sense of community. The safety net, I realized, would have to be mutualist.

Instead, for the past twenty-five years, each of us has been desperately trying to piece together our own safety net as individuals. We follow the exhortation to "invest in ourselves" by buying our own privatized health insurance and training in the form of dot-com "bootcamps," not realizing (as the Berkeley political theorist Wendy Brown has observed) that we've internalized the neoliberal idea that we are market actors first and human beings second. We save for retirement ourselves, hoping that, amid the handful of jobs we've held where our employers actually contributed to our retirement account, we will eventually cobble together enough to survive when we're older. We work short-term jobs or as solo entrepreneurs and suffer through the pain of hard times without unemployment insurance. Today, the risk that it could all come crashing down around us is not an abstract worry but a legitimate possibility. This is true for the poor, the working poor, the middle class, and the formally educated professionals—it is true for everyone outside of the tiniest fraction of our economy's top 1 percent. If you need to earn a living to provide for your family, which is true for the vast majority of us, the fact is that you are not sufficiently protected from what life might throw at you.

The decade following the 2007–2008 financial crisis saw a record-setting bull run in the stock market with unemployment at historic lows, but the statistics belied the fact that an ever-growing percentage of Americans were facing the working world entirely on their own, a fact that the chaos brought on by the COVID-19 pandemic made painfully clear. Even in 2018, 57 million Americans faced work outside a traditional employer-employee relationship, which meant many of them faced irregular income, little to no unemployment insurance or employer-sponsored health insurance, no employer-sponsored pension, and no job security. Those numbers were even more dire in 2020 and are only growing more so. In July of 2020, *The New York Times* reported that between February and May of that year, the first months of the pandemic, 5.4 million Americans lost their health insurance due to job losses. A safety net tied only to employees is useless today.

My daughter, Rachel, will soon graduate from college into a changed world. She's older than I was when I used to sit around listening to my father worry about the declining power of unions, older than my grandfather Israel was when he first joined the ILGWU. In a few years, she'll enter the workforce and, like many members of her generation, will embark on a career without any memory of a time when employers, unions, or government helped workers like her build prosperity for their families and their futures while also helping manage their risk. By 2027, a majority of Americans will be part of the independent workforce, which means a majority of Americans will be living without a safety net. Most of Rachel's peers will be freelancers, so most will be bearing their entire economic risk alone, just as she will be, in a world that will be more uncertain than ever. Most will have never belonged to a union, or even held a job that entitled them to health insurance or other fringe benefits. Rachel and her peers may simply assume that this is what work looks like: that working—and life—have always felt this precarious, this alienating, this isolating. They may simply assume that they're not entitled to the stability previous generations took for granted. They may simply assume they're not entitled to a safety net.

My entire career has been built around trying to make sure tomorrow's new workforce—workers like my daughter—understand that they are entitled to the same feeling of security that past generations have taken for granted. In 1995, I founded Working Today, the nonprofit that would become the Freelancers Union, to help create an economic infrastructure—the beginnings of a new kind of safety net—around America's newly vulnerable workforce. I wanted to build a back-to-the-future kind of labor organization, one that combined the best of the past with new technology and new organizing strategies to create a new way of thinking about benefits to protect people who had been left out of America's safety net. I spoke with countless freelancers who were all feeling the same pain: they could no longer afford health insurance. They watched prices rise every year while less and less was covered. Freelancers were forced to choose between paying astronomical individual prices for insurance and remaining uncovered, bearing tremendous personal and financial risk in the process. The Freelancers Union was able to bring elected officials together with these workers so that politicians could hear what freelancers were collectively asking for. With workers sitting at the table with policy makers, we managed to convince the New York State government to allow freelancers to be recognized as a large single group, creating a model of portable benefits that freelancers could take from job to job.

It would be years before I started to use the word "mutualism" to describe what I was building. At first, I was just following an instinct, guided by the long legacy of a life lived among worker-built institutions in the Horowitz family. But looking back, I realize I was following in a long and proud tradition of mutualist organizations in America—organizations that I began to see all around me once I knew what to look for.

The Freelancers Union was just a start. Today, more workers than ever are facing an unprecedented collapse of the safety net that they took for granted for most of their working lives. It's time to turn our attention to building a new one. My daughter, Rachel, and her generation may be graduating into a world defined by precarity, but they will also be the first adults who come of age in tomorrow's mutualist era.

What kinds of institutions will we leave them? Where will those institutions come from?

The institutions today's workforce needs must be built by workers, for workers. The safety net has always been the work of human beings, their institutions, and the social movements that deliver power to those institutions. If the history of the safety net tells us anything, it's that we are not powerless. The institutions that will support the next generation of work need to be galvanized—some built from scratch, some repurposed—and no one is going to do it for us. But by building organizations for mutual reciprocity into the communities we're already a part of, we can also build power into local markets and politics that, over time, can grow into the kind of national groundswell that will bring this new safety net to scale, as vital to the twenty-first century's workforce as the worker protections of the New Deal were in the twentieth century.

Fortunately, we have the tools we need to build them ourselves, just like my grandfather's generation did more than a century ago. It's not such a radical idea. As we'll see in the next few chapters, organizing comes naturally to us. Human beings have been practicing mutualism in every century, on every continent, for as long as society has existed. And America has a rich mutualist tradition that is older than our Constitution itself, a tradition that is as much a part of our country's identity as American capitalism and democracy. We have only to look back at the ways in which people of all cultures have come together in times of crisis to realize just how much power we hold to shape our own future.

We must become builders again. We live in a decentralized economy, and the next safety net will be no less decentralized. Traditional business and big government strategies no longer apply. We need to build tomorrow's safety net—a social contract that makes sense for our new economy—in the era we live in now. The mutualist sector, which collectively has billions and billions of dollars in revenues and employs hundreds of thousands of workers, already exists. We need to see this giant collectivity for what it is: the promise of a model for a future of shared security that rests on the institutions we've already built and will continue to build tomorrow.

CHAPTER 2

Early Mutualism

The Ism Before Capitalism

When I started building the Freelancers Union, I knew that I was following in the footsteps of my family's labor union, the ILGWU, and the worker-built safety net of the early American labor movement. But I didn't know that the ILGWU itself was part of a much larger history of mutualism that started before our country's founding—and that will continue long into the future.

As I became a collector of stories from this history, I began to see that our security has never been bought in the market or delivered only by government programs. It has always come from a shared connection and commitment to one another. The next safety net will be no different.

Mutualism didn't start with my family, the American labor movement, or even in America. I didn't coin the word "mutualism." It's not a new word or even a new idea. The practice is older, in fact, than the human race. Mutualism is a value that is so natural, and so essential to life, that the word is usually used in an entirely different context: the biological sciences.

．   ．   ．

In biology, interdependent mutualist ecosystems are every-where. Some of them are invisible: most plant species on earth exchange nutrients with underground networks of fungi in a process called mycorrhiza. But some are evident right before our eyes: every time you watch a bee pollinate a flower in your garden in exchange for the sugars in its nectar, you're watching biological mutualism. One could even argue that most life on earth began with the first mutualist ex-change. More than a billion years ago, one single-celled blob, the ancestor of every cell in your body, engulfed another, beginning the mutually beneficial relationship that under-girds almost all life on earth: that of the relationship between the cell and its energy supply, the mitochondria.

Mutualism isn't just for the fungus among us. We ourselves were mutualists before we were capitalists or socialists. As Yuval Noah Harari writes in his history of the human race, *Sapiens,* formalities like nations, governments, and markets are a shockingly recent development when seen in the context of the history of *Homo sapiens* as a species. For tens of thousands of years before the first nation was established, humans orga-nized themselves into small hunter-gatherer clans to survive—clans that many anthropologists and ethnographers have argued were remarkably cooperative and egalitarian. In the 1960s, an anthropologist named Marshall Sahlins went so far as to claim that early cooperative hunting and gathering soci-eties were the "original affluent societies." While some have since raised their eyebrows at Sahlins's idea—that early human life was rich in essential resources, relationships, and leisure time—his view hasn't gone away. In *Sapiens,* Harari speculates that a forager might have met her material needs in only three to six hours of work daily. Compare that with the typical forty-hour workweek in the developed world today, or the seventy- or eighty-hour workweeks that supposedly "affluent" American businesspeople brag about.

Is cooperation better than competition? After Darwin published *On the Origin of Species*, it became fashionable to project his theory of natural selection through competition onto all aspects of human life, especially onto capitalism. We still do this today when we describe markets and businesses using the same language we use to describe ecosystems and species—niches, competition for resources, food chains—as though economic markets and natural ecosystems are both zero-sum games. But mutualist cooperation is just as foundational to life on earth as Darwinian competition. And if humans sometimes have powerful instincts toward competition and the accumulation of power, it's worth remembering that we also have equally powerful instincts toward cooperation and egalitarianism, and we always have. Social scientists call it the "commoning" instinct, and they have observed it again and again throughout human history. A plaque in the Rochdale Pioneers Museum in England, the birthplace of the modern cooperative movement, puts it nicely: "The cooperative ideal is as old as human society. It is the idea of conflict and competition as a principle of economic progress that is new."

I've traced the first use of the word "mutualism" in a sociopolitical context to a group of French intellectuals, most notably Pierre-Joseph Proudhon (who also holds the distinction of being the first self-identified anarchist), for whom mutualism was an alternative to the revolutionary ideas of Karl Marx. The two thinkers were part of the same intellectual milieu and knew each other briefly in Paris in the early 1840s. Some scholars have even argued that Marx took his theories of surplus value, historical materialism, and class struggle almost wholly from the writings of Proudhon. Marx and Proudhon both looked at the rising tide of industrial capitalism—with its attendant inequality, deteriorating working conditions, and declining wages for industrial workers—and realized that new social movements and political ideologies would be necessary to temper capitalism's worst excesses.

But by the late 1840s, Proudhon's and Marx's ideas about how to address the rising inequality they saw around them had sharply diverged. In an 1846 letter to Marx, Proudhon wrote that he feared Marx's revolutionary ideas would succeed simply in making "ourselves the leaders of a new intolerance . . . the apostles of a new religion," and that they would produce a new order as dangerous as the old by trading out one set of orthodoxies for another. "We should not put forward *revolutionary* action as a means of social reform," Proudhon wrote, "because that pretended means would simply be an appeal to force, to arbitrariness, in brief, a contradiction." Proudhon wanted Marx to see that the revolutionary communist cure for the excesses of capitalism could be as bad as, if not worse than, the disease. Their disagreement led to what we might call a flame war today: when Proudhon published a book subtitled *The Philosophy of Poverty* in 1846, Marx shot back (a year later) with his own book, *The Poverty of Philosophy*, the title of which made it all too clear what he thought of Proudhon's ideas.

Sometimes I am asked if "mutualism" is just another word for "socialism." In reality, these two approaches to collective economics couldn't be more different. The communist and socialist wave that spread throughout the world in the twentieth century replaced capitalist markets in the only way a government can: from the top down, with blunt force and broad strokes. Proudhon, by contrast, believed that change should come from the ground up—and that government had little, if any, place in a mutualist society. Proudhon's mutualism and Marx's communism were incompatible. As one of Proudhon's followers put it, "Mutualism operates, by its very nature, to render political government, founded on arbitrary force, superfluous . . . by substituting self-government instead of government *ab extra* [from outside]."

Right here, in the difference between Marx's and Proudhon's philosophies, I see the same fight the progressive community is having today: Do you pilot nonprofit programs to determine what works and then have government impose them on the rest of the country? Or do you ask local communities what they need and then enable them to build what *they* need?

Of course, in the twentieth century Marx got the last laugh. Proudhon and his mutualism had a few adherents in the nineteenth and early twentieth centuries, but the story of the twentieth century is the story of what arose instead out of Marx's communism. Proudhon's theory of mutualism was relegated to an ideological footnote, like a branch of sociopolitical evolution that nature never explored. And since Proudhon himself was long dead by the time the Berlin Wall fell in 1989, he never got to see that he was right, after all, about one thing: the revolution came and went, and in the meantime what Proudhon feared—that communist leaders would become the "leaders of a new intolerance" based on "the religion of logic, the religion of reason"—did indeed come to pass.

Proudhon was complicated. Later in his life, he wrote things like "The Jew is the enemy of humankind. They must be sent back to Asia or be exterminated. . . . The Jew must disappear by steel or by fusion or by expulsion." Proudhon was a raving anti-Semite. But the best "fuck you" strategy, in my opinion, is usually to take someone's smartest ideas and then move on. His critique of Marx was prescient, and his alternative—mutual exchange rather than redistribution from the government—allows citizens to have more agency over their own lives. He and I look at Marx's communism from opposite ends of its history, and we both come to the same conclusion: that people are better off solving some problems on their own.

Today, with a tip of my hat to Proudhon, I'm repurposing the word "mutualism" for our future.

The use of the word "mutualism" to describe interconnected economic cooperation might date back to the nineteenth century, but the actual practice of mutualism is far older.

Just as biological mutualism coexists with Darwinian competition, so, too, has economic mutualism coexisted with economic competition (also known as capitalism) for centuries. In fact, mutualism actually predates capitalism. One of the earliest recorded instances of economic and social mutualism can be found in the very place historians credit with being the birthplace of capitalism: Amsterdam.

If, as Russell Shorto argues in *Amsterdam: A History of the World's Most Liberal City*, it was seventeenth-century Amsterdam that anchored the liberal forces that eventually produced global capitalism and the world's first experiments in democracy, then it was mutualist cooperation that produced Amsterdam in the first place. Long before René Descartes and John Locke decamped for the canal-crossed city, before the Dutch East India Company set sail from Amsterdam's ports for Asia, before Amsterdam was even a place with a name, mutualism transformed the physical landscape of the Low Countries, the loamy mess where three of Europe's largest rivers drain into the ocean, to make this part of Holland inhabitable.

It was an unlikely place for major innovation, at least on the surface. Shorto paints a loving picture of what this particular region of the world looked like prior to human settlement: "Early humans, in their migratory roaming, sensibly stepped around the whole corner of Europe known as the Low Countries. Looking at the planet not from the perspective of human beings but merely in terms of its own processes, one might say that this region was meant to be purely for drainage purposes." And yet, sometime around the turn of the first millennium, in A.D. 1000, a couple hundred farmers chose this soggy basin for their home. They settled on a marsh, and to survive they had to get creative.

First, they constructed dikes out of earth to keep the ocean waters out. Next, they drained the peat bog that remained. This left a fertile soil, which they could farm—for a little while. But there was a problem. As Shorto writes, "Once the peat loses its water it begins to sink. Eventually the peat level falls below the water level, whereupon the land is once again in danger of flooding, which necessitates more dikes as well as pumps." As soon as one area was clear of seawater and became dry enough to farm, it was already sinking and in danger of flooding all over again. To maintain their precarious perch, Holland's early farmers had to be vigilant—draining, building dikes, cutting canals, draining again, building more dikes—to keep the constant threat that the ocean would reclaim their new fertile farmland at bay. Over time, as the region became more populous, this Sisyphean task became an enormous and important responsibility that fell squarely on the shoulders of the farmers who had first settled the region.

How did they manage it? "Residents banded together to form water boards that were responsible for the complex, nonstop task of maintaining polders [reclaimed lands], dams, dikes, and water mills to keep the water at bay," Shorto writes. These boards, called *waterschappen*, were locally controlled, farmer-owned-and-operated organizations that emerged organically throughout the Netherlands as a solution to a problem that would have been far too large for any one farmer to solve on his own.

Members had duties that if shirked could result in disaster. After all, the whole region survived only by their maintaining the delicate balance between water and land. As the *waterschappen* evolved, so did their economic and organizational structures. Citizens started to pay taxes to fund the boards, and to develop rules that governed water duties, complete with punitive measures for wayward members.

It was on this Rube Goldberg machine constructed to keep nature at bay that the city of Amsterdam was eventually built. Eight centuries later, the twenty-one water authorities that continue to manage the Netherlands' canals, polders, dikes, locks, and pumping stations are the direct descendants of the *waterschappen*. According to a circular published by the Dutch water authorities in 2017, half of the land area of the Netherlands—and ten million Dutch citizens—would be underwater without them.

Hence the Dutch maxim "God made the Earth, but the Dutch made Holland." Shorto argues that it is no accident that a city built on a swamp kept afloat by independent, hardworking organizations of citizens became the hotbed of societal change and innovation that served as the cradle of early capitalism and the Enlightenment. Unlike citizens elsewhere in Europe, he writes, who owed fealty to church, class, or family, the citizens of Amsterdam found it natural to think of themselves as having agency over their own lives. There was nothing particularly earth-shattering about this idea to them: thanks to the *waterschappen,* Dutch citizens had been exerting agency over their own lives for as long as there had been people in Holland.

By the early nineteenth century, these Enlightenment ideas had made their way to another outpost in an unlikely place: America. We tend to think of the story of America as the story of the triumph of capitalism. But in our nation's earliest years, mutualist economic activity was what allowed average citizens to live rich lives.

Alexis de Tocqueville, the son of a French nobleman, was only twenty-five years old when he and his best friend, Gustave de Beaumont, set sail for America in 1831. The observations he made—collected a few years later in *Democracy in America*—remain among the richest portraits we have of our young nation. The world was changing: All across Europe, the old world of kings and noblemen was giving way to something new. Mercantilism, the economic system that had ruled the European continent for centuries, was being replaced by the earliest rumblings of capitalism. And democracy, a form of government almost unheard of only fifty or so years prior, was ascendant. Nowhere were these new ideas more exuberantly realized than in America.

What impressed Tocqueville even more than our government or our economy was our tendency to instinctively and organically organize ourselves into groups, which was something he had never seen before:

In America I encountered sorts of associations of which, I confess, I had no idea. Americans of all ages, all conditions, all minds, constantly unite. Not only do they have commercial and industrial associations in which all take part, but they also have a thousand other kinds: religious, moral, grave, futile, very general and very particular, immense and very small; Americans use associations to give fêtes, to found seminaries, to build inns, to raise churches, to distribute books, to send missionaries to the antipodes; in this manner they create hospitals, prisons, schools.

"Associations." This was Tocqueville's word for groups of people who had a problem to solve and who realized that working together was the most efficient way to solve it. They didn't have a choice: America's fledgling capitalist economy was mostly confined to coastal cities and port towns, which had become thriving marketplaces full of wealthy and cosmopolitan people from all over the world doing business with one another. But this robust economic activity was barely evident in the rural interior of America. To the extent that capitalism existed outside of major cities at all, it was local to the point of being home-brewed—a cobbler would sell his wares to a neighbor, a baker would buy flour from a neighbor—but this intimate system of economic connections would rarely touch the world outside the villages where these people lived. Before good roads, before cars or airplanes, before any kind of communication was possible except by letter, rural America in the early 1800s was even more cut off from the country's urban centers than it is today.

So how did people survive? They passed around the collection hat at church; they collectively built schools; they banded together and set out for the West. There wasn't anything but pragmatism behind these choices: in an era before the U.S. government or the tendrils of market forces had penetrated America's hinterlands, "associations" were simply the best way for most Americans to solve their most basic problems. "Everywhere that, at the head of a new undertaking you see the government in France and a great lord in England, count on it that you will perceive an association in the United States," Tocqueville wrote. Americans helped themselves, and this was what set our country apart.

Tocqueville's "associations" are just one of the first examples of a tendency that has united Americans since this country's inception: our impulse to come together in times of need. Early America offered particularly rich soil for mutualist experimentation because America was an experiment itself. The radical Enlightenment idea—that human beings could be more than their class or birth destined them to be, and could instead exert meaningful control over their own lives—had a powerful influence on our Founding Fathers, but it also had a profound effect on common people everywhere. For the first time, ordinary citizens were realizing that they could take their destinies into their own hands and work together to find novel solutions to the problem of how to live a better life.

We can trace the origins of modern insurance to some of America's earliest associations. Benjamin Franklin's Philadelphia Contributionship for the Insurance of Houses from Loss by Fire, founded in 1752, arose out of another association, also one of Franklin's social inventions: the Union Fire Company (informally, the Bucket Brigade), one of the first all-volunteer fire departments in America, founded in 1736. To join the Philadelphia Contributionship, members contributed equally to a fund that would be paid out to any member whose property was damaged by fire. They signed up for this insurance for a period of seven years, and at the end of that time the money they contributed would be returned to them. During the first year, 143 such policies were written. Franklin envisioned similar arrangements of mutual insurance in other sectors of life: insurance for widows or orphans, life insurance, even crop insurance. It is from Franklin's Philadelphia Contributionship that we get two essential features of all modern insurance policies: the idea of rating risk, and the necessity of having large pools of capital on hand, called reserves, to fund payouts. The idea was basic and communitarian: life is risky, so let's distribute the risk as broadly as possible so that no one is ever too exposed.

Of course, buying insurance was a luxury many Americans couldn't afford. Indeed, early American capitalism was built on the backs of enslaved Blacks, the descendants of whom continue to be left out of the American dream today. But even for the Black community, "associations" proved to be a bulwark against risk. On April 12, 1787, Absalom Jones and Richard Allen, two former slaves who had risen to prominence as ministers in Philadelphia, resolved to create the Free African Society, an organization in which "free Africans and their descendants" could come together to support one another in times of need.

Originally conceived as a nondenominational place for Blacks to worship, the Free African Society was a mutual aid society that helped give structural and financial support to those who were sick or had otherwise fallen on hard times. Members paid a subscription to the society, which would go to help the most vulnerable. "We . . . do unanimously agree," their founding document read, ". . . to advance one shilling in silver Pennsylvania currency a month; and after one year's subscription from the date hereof, then to hand forth to the needy of this Society, if any should require, the sum of three shillings and nine pence per week of the said money . . . and if any should neglect paying his monthly subscription for three months . . . he shall be disjointed from us, by being informed by two of the members as an offender, without having any of his subscription money returned." It was one of the first of what would become a remarkable array of mutual aid societies in the Black community that allowed both free and enslaved Blacks to exert some measure of self-determination during the eighteenth and nineteenth centuries, even in a country that actively excluded them from its protections. It not only laid the groundwork for a long history of mutual aid that helped Blacks self-organize, worship, and care for one another—a history that can be traced from slavery up through the civil rights era—but it also served as the basis of two of the first Black churches—the African Episcopal Church and the African Methodist Episcopal Church—in America. Out of these early "associations," the Black community built the mutualist groundwork that allowed them to get their social and economic needs met, even in the most hostile of environments.

Utopian societies, America's most successful experiments in mutualist economics, date back to the same time period as Tocqueville's "associations." This widespread experiment in communal living in rural America began in the 1780s and peaked in the mid-1800s. These Utopias, which have entered our history books mainly as curiosities, varied widely in their leadership styles, organizing principles, and views on sex. But they all had one thing in common that the history books largely ignore: a damn good, scalable business model. The communities were made up mostly of average citizens looking for ways to lead a better life. And by building communal societies around mutual exchange, they succeeded to a remarkable extent. Rather than looking at these Utopian communities through the lens of their social arrangements—which were, admittedly, sometimes a little weird—let's consider the economic mechanism at their heart.

Officially organized in 1787 in New Lebanon, New York, the Shakers were the oldest, longest-running, and most successful of the American Utopians. At the movement's height in the mid-nineteenth century, there were nineteen Shaker societies stretching from Maine to Kentucky, containing in aggregate as many as six thousand members, who owned tens of thousands of acres of land. We owe the hymn "Simple Gifts" to the Shakers, a fitting anthem for these modest, pious people, who were plain in all things. Unlike other settlers in America, whose households were occupied, on average, by only two productive adults, the Shakers lived communally. A Shaker community contained several "families," each of which could be considered a small mutualist enterprise unto itself. Family members lived in a simple, large, well-built house capable of accommodating as many as ninety men and women, who slept in dormitory-style cot beds. The sexes were separated by a wide hall, and children (many of them orphans from surrounding areas) were raised by the community. The Shakers' style of dress was so simple and uniform that a casual observer would have had difficulty distinguishing between the young and the old.

The Shakers' communal approach to living—not to mention a strict adherence to celibacy—meant that more got done, and more efficiently. They rose early, worked hard, and lived plain and unadorned lives. Above all, they valued thrift, simplicity, and honesty. They believed that God was manifest in the smallest details of their work, and they produced goods of the finest quality, distinguished by a clean design and an emphasis on utility. These goods, especially their furniture, were real works of art. In an era in which mass production was otherwise associated with shoddiness, the Shakers made sturdy, elegant, mass-produced tables, chairs, and other furniture.

But the Shakers were also shrewd businesspeople, and their collectivity was their special sauce. By pooling their labor, they could leapfrog over most Americans who worked in isolated households to eke out a living. They could afford new technology, pioneer or borrow production techniques to improve their output, and keep their expenses—both for household needs and for tools—down through economies of scale. They eagerly participated in markets, selling furniture and the yields from their fields. Eventually, through doing business with the outside world, the Shakers amassed enough capital to invest in more land, which allowed them to grow their businesses even further.

The sheer scale and industry of the Shaker movement was remarkable: Shaker furniture today has a place in New York City's Metropolitan Museum of Art, which calls the Shakers "the largest and most successful communal experiment in American history." I'll second that and add this: the Shakers were one of the most successful mutualist organizations ever in America. They lasted, in one form or another, for two hundred years, which is something that can't be said for even the most successful American corporations.

Yet the Shakers weren't alone. Other Utopian societies included the Perfectionists of Oneida, New York; the Harmonists at Economy, in western Pennsylvania; the Amana Colonies in Iowa; and Zoar in Ohio. Karl Marx was even influenced by these early Utopian communes (hence the commune-ists!).

A journalist named Charles Nordhoff took it upon himself to explore these Utopian communities at their height in the 1870s, when there were seventy-two communes in thirteen states. The communes offered a path to prosperity for people from America's hinterlands who would never have been able to break into the elite centers of early capitalism in America's major cities—a chance to compete economically with the shrewdest businesspeople in America. Nordhoff wrote, "It is probably a low estimate of the wealth of the seventy-two communes to place it at twelve millions of dollars." That would be close to $280 million in 2021.

But it wasn't just their wealth that impressed him. During the accumulation of that wealth, Nordhoff wrote, America's Utopias "enjoyed a greater amount of comfort, and vastly greater security against want and demoralization, than were attained by their neighbors or the surrounding population, with better schools and opportunities of training for their children, and far less exposure for the women, and the aged and infirm. . . . To be fairly judged, the communal life . . . must be compared with that of the mechanic and laborer in our cities, and of the farmer in the country; and thus when put in judgement, I do not hesitate to say that it is in many ways and in almost all ways—a higher and better, and also a

pleasanter life." In other words, the communities were building an early safety net for their members.

Those earliest days of American cooperation set the stage for
centuries of remarkable mutualist innovation. Associations
like the ones Tocqueville identified were the antecedents of a
whole sector of communal approaches to living, lending,
saving, buying, working, banking, insuring, housing, farming,
and caring that have existed throughout our country's history, many of which are still part of our economy today. Mutualism is deeply American, from Benjamin Franklin's first
all-volunteer fire brigade, founded in 1736; to the Utopian
experiments of the nineteenth century; to other examples I'll
explore later in this book—the rich and complex network of
mutual aid societies developed by African Americans beginning during slavery and lasting through Jim Crow and the
civil rights era; the golden age of unions that my grandfather
helped usher in; and the massive agricultural cooperatives
that still power much of our economy today. It is possible to
look at the history of our country not just as the history of
democratic government or capitalist markets, but rather as
the history of all the ways people have come together to solve
their own problems since America's founding.

So if the tradition of mutualism runs like a bright line
through the history of our country, why is it so hard for us to
see it today?

As in the fable of the blind men and the elephant, one
reason is that when we look at the history of our country, we
often see only parts of the whole: Franklin's early insurance
experiments, the early Black church, the Utopians; later, labor
unions, cooperative grocery stores and housing, or urban mu-

tual aid. Each is an institution that exists for a social purpose, has an economic mechanism that sustains it, and is built to outlast its members. We're really talking about the same thing: the myriad ways people come together to help one another. Without the frame of mutualism, it's hard to recognize how much each of these organizations have in common.

But we've also lost sight of the mutualist sector because, since the 1970s, it has been hollowed out by sabotage on the right and neglect on the left. The right eviscerated unions in the service of market efficiency; the left split the working class in two and began to see government as the only means of effecting real social change. The power of community has been forgotten, and this has caused us to lose track of this third thread in American economic life. It is only in the past few years, through a resurgence of interest in the labor movement and mutual aid among young progressives, that some Americans have learned that once, not so long ago, these organizations were an essential part of how we took care of one another.

I'm not the first person to make this observation. In recent years, a number of books have identified the blind spot that we've collectively developed for community institutions of all kinds. Yuval Levin's books *A Time to Build* and *The Fractured Republic* have made the argument that American life actually occurs in the space between the state and the individual. In *America Beyond Capitalism,* Gar Alperovitz sees the potential for a future of shared prosperity in an idea he calls the "Pluralist Commonwealth." Raghuram Rajan's *The Third Pillar* correctly makes the argument that seeing society as having only to do with a relationship between markets and governments leaves out an important "third pillar" of our social and economic lives.

But it was Robert Putnam who articulated these ideas first and best in his landmark study of civic and social organizations in the United States, *Bowling Alone,* published in 2000. In it, Putnam charts the influence of this third pillar of American life throughout our history and chronicles its steady decline. Putnam recognized that organizations like bowling leagues, PTAs, churches, local political organizations, VFWs, Black churches, and even fraternal organizations and country clubs all rely on what he calls social capital. "Social capital," he writes, "refers to connections among individuals—social networks and the norms of reciprocity and trustworthiness that arise from them." Not only does social capital keep these organizations functioning by creating a culture of trust and reciprocity, but joining and engaging with such organizations increases the social capital of their members. These kinds of organizations, Putnam argues, form an essential bedrock of American social life. In their absence, we all just end up bowling alone.

Putnam sees social capital at work in American society across many kinds of institutions: through politics and political parties, through what he calls civic associations, through churches and unions, and through more informal avenues (he gives the example of a group of co-workers getting together for drinks after work, or even a simple nod to a fellow runner you see every day in the park). But social capital is just a start.

Mutualist organizations go one step further by *using* the strong connections between their members to work together economically to support their social purpose to solve problems.

Today, Tocqueville's "associations" have matured into four principal types of mutualist organizations that do just this, and that continue to drive parts of the American economy: religious organizations, mutual aid societies, cooperatives, and labor organizations. (We'll explore the role that each of these parts of the contemporary mutualist sector continues to play in the economy today in the pages to come.) The membership numbers and reach of these sectors of the economy are huge. Ten million Americans are covered by fourteen hundred unionized pension fund plans, and there is $197 billion in the agricultural sector of the cooperative movement alone. Mutualism works—it scales. It's just that we've forgotten how to build mutualist organizations.

Once we recognize the mutualist sector for what it really is—a massive sector of the economy that already changes the lives of people in real, day-to-day ways—government can step into its next role: supporting and scaling the mutualist sector through policy tools like tax codes, zoning ordinances, and insurance regulation. We can build it into a great mosaic of institutions that will make up the safety net that tomorrow's workforce will so desperately need: health clinics, education centers, lending circles, mutual insurance, affordable cooperative housing, and more. When we do this, we'll be building on a long and proud history that is not only deeply American but also deeply human.

But first, we have to learn to recognize a mutualist organization when we see one. When we do, we can find our own place in this movement and start making our own contribution to tomorrow's safety net.

CHAPTER 3

Mutualist Organization

The Three Rules of Mutualism

O nce I began to see mutualism for what it is—a sector of the economy that has existed for hundreds of years—I started to see it all around me. Today, it is alive and well in the form of religious organizations, mutual aid societies, cooperatives, and labor unions.

These mutualist organizations are already how we're solving problems in our own lives. In the worst moments of the COVID-19 pandemic, drive-in and virtual religious services kept people socially connected; local mutual aid societies helped neighborhoods care for their own; cooperative groceries kept communities fed; unions stood up to companies that asked their workers to return to work too soon. These organizations are uniquely positioned to deliver tomorrow's safety net. But before we can build new mutualist organizations into our communities, we need to learn to recognize mutualism when we see it.

How?

I've been immersed in the mutualist sector for twenty-five

years, and in that time I've identified three characteristics that all mutualist organizations have in common, from the most modest informal mutual aid societies to the most sophisticated cooperatives and labor unions.

1. Mutualist organizations have a **social purpose:** to solve a social problem for a community. A mutualist organization exists to serve its members, not to make a profit.
2. Mutualist organizations must have an independent, sustainable **economic mechanism.** Revenues must exceed expenses. In other words, a mutualist organization must have a way of making money.
3. Mutualist organizations have a **long-term focus.** They are intergenerational institutions with leadership infrastructures and capital strategies that equip them to serve future generations. They are built to outlast their members.

Let's take a closer look at each one.

The Three Principles of Mutualism

1. Mutualist organizations have a social purpose: to solve a social problem for a community.

The true heart of any mutualist organization lies in its social purpose and the community it serves. That social purpose can be grand—for example, to try to improve the lives of tens of thousands of garment workers on the Lower East Side—or it can be something as modest as improving access to affordable groceries for a local community. It can be something utilitarian, like keeping your land from flooding, or it could be something convenient: REI is a consumer cooperative that makes outdoor gear affordable and easy to return for its customers. Or it can be existential: Black churches, Black mutual aid societies, and Black cooperatives in the eighteenth, nineteenth, and early twentieth centuries helped the Black community survive, and in some cases thrive, in the face of oppression.

There's a natural tendency to look at these examples and make judgments about each one's value, but I take an intentionally broad view of what counts as a social purpose. In each of these cases, a community wanted an organization to exist that wouldn't have existed if it were up to government or markets alone. So the community members found a way to build—and then protect, nurture, and grow—the organization they wanted or needed. Mutualism was the tool.

Ask yourself what problems need solving in your own life, and don't worry if the answers you come up with sound small. There is no hierarchy of social purpose. As we'll see throughout this book, the grandest and most important social movements in America have started with people asking themselves what problems need to be solved in their own lives.

First, identify and connect with other people who experience the same problems as you. In labor law, we call the group of people you find and organize with your *community of interest*. A community of interest can be organized around a community, concern, skill, shared location, or trade. For a labor union, a community of interest might be, say, autoworkers in Detroit. For a church, a community of interest is a congregation. A local food co-op's community of interest is people who want access to good, affordable food in their own neighborhood. Recent immigrants to the United States often form mutual aid societies to help one another get started in America. This is as true for immigrants today who work together to support a new arrival who wants to start a business such as a corner deli or greengrocer as it was for Jewish garment workers in the 1910s and 1920s.

How do you keep a mutualist organization from tipping over into that other ism that is far too common today: tribalism? There's no easy answer, but the key is this: Mutualist organizations are built on trust, not fear. They are about building, not tearing down. While there is nothing wrong with wanting to break bread with people who see things the same way you do, when the institution you form becomes about exclusion rather than cooperation, you've stopped practicing mutualism.

In his discussion of social capital, Robert Putnam makes a distinction between two kinds of social capital that I find useful: *bridging*, or inclusive social capital, and *bonding*, or exclusive social capital. Those who practice *bridging* look for ways to connect. They are part of a group whose dynamics are oriented outward, not inward—toward inclusivity and connection with other institutions. Those who practice *bonding* reinforce insularity, balkanization, and social alienation. This is where too much of our politics lives today: we participate in groups, but we talk among ourselves. Mutualism is about building, not tearing down, so truly mutualist organizations are built on bridging, not bonding, social capital. Not every mutualist organization is perfect in this regard. To be sure, the history of the labor movement is full of examples of organizations built around exclusion. But history has also shown that even the most exclusive mutualist organizations have tended, over the course of their existence, toward inclusion and connection. As we'll see later in this book, even the racist and parochial elements of the American Federation of Labor (AFL) didn't stop it from eventually becoming a significant supporter of civil rights.

But mutualism also is self-help, not charity. For that reason, its community must have the ability to make decisions independently. To do that, it needs cash.

2. Mutualist organizations must have an independent, sustainable economic mechanism.

Existing for a social purpose doesn't mean that money doesn't change hands. It can, and in fact it should. Any truly mutualist organization must have an economic mechanism that participates in markets to ensure that the organization will survive. The difference is that the economic activity is not solely determined by the pressures of the market. It is, instead, dictated by the needs of the organization's community of interest, and it exists to fund that organization's social purpose.

When I say "economic mechanism," I really just mean a way of making money. A mutualist organization needs to have money coming in, and it needs to have more money coming in than it has going out. This economic mechanism doesn't have to be fancy, sophisticated, or innovative. After all, the goal of a mutualist organization isn't to invent new business models or disrupt sectors of the economy. The goal is to have enough money to fund its social purpose and ensure its longevity. (As blockchain, the type of distributed ledger technology used by the cryptocurrency Bitcoin, starts to get used in the social sector more, I believe the idea of exchange will eventually evolve to include nonmonetary forms of reciprocal exchange as well.)

Unions, other labor organizations, and many professional associations fund their social purpose by collecting dues from their members. Food co-ops like the Park Slope Food Coop in Brooklyn, New York, fund their social purpose by selling food (at a deep discount, but with enough of a margin that it covers their operating expenses), charging new members $125 to buy in, and relying on member labor. The Freelancers Union funds its organizing efforts and advocacy for freelancers by selling insurance to its members as an insurance broker. Organizations like the Elks and Rotary charge dues. Newer communities like those that organize through Patreon or Substack operate on a subscription model. Community spaces like the Brooklyn Botanic Garden rent out their spaces for weddings. Even neighborhood theater groups sell tickets. Tried-and-true business models like subscriptions, ticket sales, rentals (of equipment or space), selling services, and sponsorships are a great place to start. The important thing is that money is coming in and that you have a plan for what to do with it.

The key here is that the economic mechanism must be *independent and sustainable* and also connected to the community the organization serves. The way that a mutualist organization funds itself must begin and end with the organization itself, rather than with any third party. This is essential. In this way, the organization retains complete decision-making authority and remains answerable only to its community of interest. Wealthy donors and charities may use their capital to do good in the world, but since the decisions about what causes to fund necessarily come from the person or organization doing the funding rather than the community of interest whose lives that money affects, such charities and foundations are not mutualist. Perhaps one reason that the mutualist sector in America has not been replenished in decades is that this notion scares people: true mutualism cedes decision-making authority to the communities it serves by giving them economic power, and therefore takes that power away from those used to being in control. We'll need to build new ways for these communities to get the financing they need so that they can build lasting independence and power far into the future.

3. Mutualist organizations have a long-term focus.

Consider the idea, often attributed to the Great Law of Peace, the oral constitution of the Iroquois Confederacy, that any wise decision must take into account the welfare of those living seven generations in the future. It's a striking idea because it is so different from how most of us live our lives, and equally different from how most corporations conduct business. Most of us don't plan for our own obsolescence, and the CEO of a conventional corporation is answerable first and foremost to the board of directors and shareholders at the end of every quarter, so maximizing short-term profits becomes the priority.

A healthy mutualist organization must try to plan for at least two generations in the future. How? The organization can't rely on the leadership of a single charismatic, intelligent, or innovative founder. It must, instead, create a self-reliant institution that is bigger than any one person. It can do this by creating offices (president, treasurer, and so on) that outlive the people who occupy them, or by creating a board of directors (made up of the organization's members), which confers decision-making authority to a group. Some mutualist organizations, especially cooperatives, even adopt a set of principles to guide them: a founder may die or move on, but the principles that define the institution live on.

Decoupling an institution from a single founding individual doesn't mean doing away with leadership. To the contrary, a mutualist organization must get comfortable with the idea of leadership if it is to survive, whether that leadership is in the form of an elected president, a board, a set of guiding principles, or some combination of all of these. Why is leadership so important? One of the key aspects of a mutualist organization is its ability to self-determine. Without leadership, it's impossible for the organization to make adult decisions about where its money does or doesn't go. A mutualist organization's leader or leaders should be held accountable by the community of interest, and structures should be put in place to allow for the transmission of knowledge from one generation to the next. Hierarchy in a mutualist organization exists not only to facilitate decision-making but also to provide a path toward leadership—and a way to transmit the organization's core values and mission—for a new generation.

To plan for the long term, mutualist organizations also need to take a long-range financial view by making investments that ensure they will continue to exist to serve future generations. When I started building the Freelancers Union, I was surprised by just how hard this is to do. Mutualist organizations today are starved for capital that can help them build or expand, because they need a kind of investment—an investment of patient capital—that just doesn't exist.

What do I mean by "patient capital"? All monetary exchanges, from financial gifts (investments made with an expectation of a 0 percent return over an indefinite time period) to usury (predatory loans made with interest rates so high that the borrower will be in debt indefinitely), exist on a spectrum along which the variable that changes is the rate of return. Between these two extremes is every form of economic activity you can imagine—from foundation grants and Section 8 public housing to your neighborhood check-cashing place and the aggressive investments of Fortune 500 companies and venture capitalists.

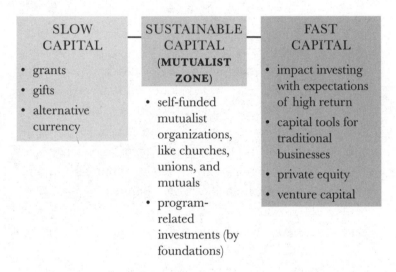

SLOW CAPITAL	SUSTAINABLE CAPITAL (MUTUALIST ZONE)	FAST CAPITAL
• grants • gifts • alternative currency	• self-funded mutualist organizations, like churches, unions, and mutuals • program-related investments (by foundations)	• impact investing with expectations of high return • capital tools for traditional businesses • private equity • venture capital

We call these categories of monetary exchange *capital markets*, which is just another way of talking about where the money comes from. If you want to do something that requires capital, who is going to loan you a big chunk of money to do it, and what are they going to expect in return? Most of capitalism occurs toward the right side of this graph: fast capital and investments expected to produce huge returns in a few years (as in the case of a Silicon Valley startup). Most charity occurs toward the left side. In the middle is a section that is curiously empty in the twenty-first century—sustainable capital: investments that will reliably make money but aren't going to make anyone obscenely rich over a short period of time. This is the mutualist zone. One of the only forms of patient lending available in today's capital markets is mortgages, which is why one of the first things many sophisticated mutualist organizations do is get a loan to buy a building. Otherwise, progressive capital markets—where investing meets social purpose—are almost impossible to find.

So mutualist organizations also plan for the future by investing in themselves. They do this by *recycling excess capital* generated by their economic mechanism back into the organization. One type of organization that recycles excess capital all the time is an endowment—an organization that makes investments and then reinvests a certain portion of the returns back into the endowment, growing it over time. But you don't have to have a billion-dollar endowment, as many universities do, to recycle capital effectively. You just need to recognize that any extra money in a mutualist organization is for the community the organization serves, and the best way the community can use that money is in ways that will perpetuate the organization's continued existence. This could be through traditional investments, as in the case of a university's endowment, or it could be through a more general investment in the future, such as saving up to purchase a building for the organization, investing in relevant training for members, or putting the money in a pot set aside for members to use in case of emergency. What matters most is that when you have more money than you expect to, you use it to plan for the community's future.

A mutualist organization is always planting saplings that its founders will never see grow into mature trees. The shade of those trees is for the next generation.

The Mutualist Safety Net

How can we use the mutualist sector to build tomorrow's safety net?

Let's start by considering what the safety net really is. It's a series of jobs: someone has to have the job of delivering health, dental, disability, and life insurance; someone has to have the job of opening health clinics; someone has to have the job of helping people save for retirement; someone has to train and educate workers in skills that will help them keep up.

In 1935, Franklin Roosevelt gave unions a job: to collectively bargain for higher wages. But what if we give other kinds of institutions jobs as well?

Mutualist institutions perform many of these jobs already. Religious institutions have wide networks of social services. Mutual aid societies originated insurance, but today they also help communities get access to basic services. Cooperatives provide affordable groceries to communities living in food deserts and undergird our agricultural sector. Unions negotiate for high-quality, finely tuned insurance plans that serve their members' unique and sometimes idiosyncratic needs.

The mutualist sector is uniquely positioned to deliver tomorrow's safety net, if we can leverage it. It not only has the experience to do this, but it also has the resources. The mutualist sector is huge, if we know how to spot it, and already touches millions of lives.

Religious Organizations

Whatever your views about the role of religion in society, or about faith itself, one thing is undeniably true: the faith community knows something about generating revenue to support a social purpose that reaches a wide community. A 2016 study by the *Interdisciplinary Journal of Research on Religion,* cited in *The Guardian,* estimated that over 150 million Americans belong to close to 345,000 congregations, which themselves collectively spend tens of billions of dollars building social programs and services, for a combined value of almost $1.3 trillion a year (which would make the U.S. religious sector the same size as the fifteenth-largest economy in the world).

Religious institutions have always been some of the most powerful incubators of mutualist activity. After all, religion gives us the world's first labor story: Exodus. Pharaoh was the first bad boss, Moses was the first labor leader, and the Exodus was the first strike. Self-organization is even coded into the DNA of the Jewish faith: many religious ceremonies and obligations require a minimum of ten adults, called a minyan (it used to be a minimum of ten *men*), to be present before public prayer can occur. Your local church, synagogue, mosque, or other religious community is a sophisticated mutualist organization hiding in plain sight. The Catholic Church even put a name to its own unique brand of mutualism: subsidiarity, the belief that a central governing authority should always take a back seat in making decisions that can be made locally.

It's no accident that some of the mutualist organizations we've already explored come out of religious communities. From the Free African Society and the Utopias of the nineteenth century to the Jewish trade unions of the early twentieth century, communities based on religion and religious culture are dry tinder for the mutualist spark. The contemporary religious right has also demonstrated just how powerful mutualism can be at scale: megachurches and other conservative Christian groups exert an outsized influence on politics and policy in America.

We already turn to our communities of faith in times of need. Religious organizations already deliver a significant portion of the safety net to their communities: education, insurance, even at one point housing and orphanages. Religious organizations play an especially outsized role in the healthcare industry. In fact, about 18.5 percent of all hospitals are religiously affiliated, especially with the Catholic Church.

The religious sector has several elements that the organizations that will deliver the next safety net will need: a hyperlocal focus on the needs of a community, expertise, and a social purpose mission that puts its members first. Religious communities already have their own physical and civic infrastructure: experts in finance, healthcare, insurance, real estate, and more. What if we leveraged that infrastructure to do even more?

Mutual Aid Societies

As soon as the pandemic hit, mutual aid societies sprang up across the globe. There was no dress rehearsal, no how-to video that everybody could watch. Instead, the impulse to help one another and to seek connection during a time of stress came naturally to people. Sophisticated and robust mutual aid societies—scaled and made efficient through the smart use of technology platforms like Google Groups, Slack, and Airtable—appeared with breathtaking speed in New York City neighborhoods such as Williamsburg, Prospect–Lefferts Gardens, Crown Heights, Fort Greene, Morningside Heights, and Harlem. But the magic wasn't in the technology; it was in the connection and love that emerged among people who had, until then, been perfect strangers. For the first time in my life, I saw people making their own decisions about whether to take their kids out of school, whether to take public transportation, whether to self-quarantine in the face of contradictory advice and leadership. Federal leadership was gone, and as a society we stepped forward into this abyss with an outpouring of mutualist activity that was as necessary as it was spontaneous.

Mutual aid is nothing new. Mutual aid societies are one of the most basic and enduring forms of mutualism. They can be as small as a hyper-local grocery drop or as sophisticated as Ben Franklin's early insurance companies. Some insurance companies, such as State Farm, still remain mutualized today. According to the International Cooperative and Mutual Insurance Federation, in 2017 the biggest mutual cooperative insurers wrote $1.2 trillion worth of policies worldwide. Between these two poles of complexity are an array of mutual aid organizations that serve a constituency as diverse as America itself.

The best examples of mutual aid societies today can be found in immigrant communities, which often use a special kind of mutual aid called a *lending circle* to help defray the costs of members getting on their feet in a new country, including obtaining immigration paperwork, getting a loan to start a business, or putting down a deposit to rent an apartment. This relatively simple financial arrangement makes saving or borrowing for a major purchase accessible to new immigrants who might not have a credit score or even a bank account. Called tontines, kyes, huays, tandas, or chit funds depending on the community, lending circles work like this: A group of, say, ten people each contribute $100 to the lending circle every month. The first month, one of those ten people gets $1,000, the total of the ten members' contributions. The next month, someone else gets the same payout. At month ten, the last person takes the $1,000, and the circle begins again. A 2013 article in *The Atlantic* explains it this way: "In a lending circle, the first person to receive the lump sum acts like a borrower: He's given money that he repays in installments. But the last person acts like a saver: He puts away small sums of money and gets it all back at the end. Everyone in between acts like a lender and takes their turn at being the borrower."

Mutual aid societies are among the simplest and therefore most agile and widespread forms of mutualism, filling vacuums in need in communities large and small all over the world. While one of their strengths is that they begin with the kind of informal structure that lets them spring up overnight in the wake of a crisis, as they grow they begin to plan for the long term by forming a board of directors, electing officers, putting leadership structures in place, and creating reserves of capital to ensure they aren't a flash in the pan.

But what if these agile, hyper-local mutualist organizations were given the tools and the opportunity to scale? What more could they be doing to help communities build their own safety net?

Cooperatives

Cooperatives are a huge sector of the American economy hiding in plain sight. The total gross business volume of agricultural cooperatives—in which farmers share the costs of the major capital investments required for farming at scale (seeds, tractors, threshers, other machinery)—alone was about $197 billion, with about $93 billion in total assets, in 2017. Worldwide, cooperativism is even bigger. According to the International Co-operative Alliance, there are around three million cooperatives in the world, and 12 percent of all human beings are part of some kind of cooperative.

In addition to agricultural cooperatives, there are *purchasing cooperatives*, which small businesses join to improve their buying power; *utility cooperatives*, utility companies that are owned by communities in rural regions of the United States for which buying utilities from a for-profit corporation would be prohibitively expensive; *housing cooperatives*, some union sponsored, like the one my grandmother lived in; *banking cooperatives*, like credit unions and other financial institutions that exist primarily to serve communities rather than to make outsized returns; *retail cooperatives*, stores owned by their customers; and *worker cooperatives*, like the small worker-owned shop near Manchester, England, that started the cooperative movement.

That's right: the entire cooperative sector can be traced to a single location—the ground floor of 31 Toad Lane in the town of Rochdale, near Manchester, where in 1844 twenty-eight weavers pooled their resources and opened a shop that sold staples such as sugar, butter, flour, oatmeal, and candles at reasonable prices. Known as the Rochdale Society of Equitable Pioneers, the weavers were so poor at first that they had to use bars and planks to construct a shop counter and bench for customers, but they had a vision: by opening a business that existed for the sole purpose of solving a social problem—that is, the need for affordable, high-quality food and essential goods—they could put themselves on a path to a better life.

Previous attempts elsewhere to start worker cooperatives

had largely failed (early co-ops let members run up tabs, for example, rather than demanding full payment at the time of purchase). The Pioneers, by contrast, were guided from the very beginning by a set of principles to govern their daily activities and decision-making. Without knowing it, they were forming the bedrock of the modern cooperative movement. By 1863, 332 cooperatives were operating in the UK, following the Rochdale model. By the early twentieth century, thousands of similar co-ops existed in the UK and around the world. Over time, the original "objects" of the pioneers were expanded into a set of seven principles—the Rochdale Principles—that continue to be a North Star for almost all cooperatives worldwide: voluntary and open membership; democratic member control; member economic participation; autonomy and independence; education, training, and information; cooperation among cooperatives; and concern for community.

Today, the cooperative sector that grew out of these seven principles is all around us. Common consumer brands and retailers—including Land O'Lakes, Ace Hardware, Organic Valley, Ocean Spray, Sunkist Growers, Cabot Creamery, REI, and the Green Bay Packers—are all cooperatives of one sort or another. Cooperative energy companies, from rural energy cooperatives to new, forward-looking companies like Namasté Solar in Colorado, power much of America's electrical grid. Other cooperatives—like NannyBee in Manhattan and Cooperative Home Care Associates in the Bronx, which is the largest worker-owned cooperative in the United States—are finding new ways to deliver essential services such as childcare and home healthcare while also raising the quality of life of their workers. The New School in New York City hosts the Platform Cooperativism Consortium, which provides resources for the vast global community of platform-based cooperatives to help meet the needs of the evolving digital transformation of cooperatives.

Cooperatives have vast financial infrastructures and knowledge, and they are built around the mission of providing for their communities. The U.S. Federation of Worker Cooperatives and the National Cooperative Business Association are two examples of sophisticated organizations that undergird the cooperative field. Cooperatives are robust economic entities that operate with sophisticated technologies for the good of a community, which situates them perfectly to deliver the next safety net.

Labor Organizations

Unions remain a huge sector of the American economy. Despite the fact that for decades pundits have declared that labor is dead, today more than fourteen million Americans are union members. (Pundits in the 1920s also declared that labor was dead, only to be proven wrong in the 1930s and 1940s.) Today, labor is again experiencing a resurgence in public support, and the modern labor movement is leveraging technology to reach a whole new constituency. Digital workplaces like Kickstarter, BuzzFeed, and Gimlet have started to unionize, and teachers' unions in West Virginia and elsewhere have used the power of social media to draw attention to their causes.

Tomorrow's labor movement won't be monolithic. But neither was yesterday's. Unions have always been varied, ranging from craft unions (focused on a particular skill, such as bricklaying), to industrial unions (focused on an entire industry, such as automakers), to public sector unions (focused on local, state, and federal workers). Today, we're adding new types of unions that I call "network unions," representing independent contractors, such as Rideshare Drivers United and the Freelancers Union, and even some organizations, like the freelance writers' listserv Study Hall, that don't call themselves unions but operate like the best of them.

Unions have built America's safety net not once but twice: first in the Progressive Era of the 1910s and '20s, and then again after the New Deal through the 1950s and '60s. Today, they continue to have significant civic, physical, and economic infrastructure, plus a track record of building local mutualist organizations that ladder up into the vast network of the larger trade union movement. They know how to rally their members, how to build, how to exercise their power to win workplace protections, and how to lobby for widespread social legislation. But most important, the safety net they provide is built to serve their members, who trust them to know what workers need better than anyone else. Mine workers' unions, for instance, negotiate to make sure that their members' health insurance plans cover black lung. Entertainment and building trade unions have piloted important forms of portable benefits, as have public sector unions, which have enabled federal employees to take their benefits from job to job. Unions have been and can again be one of the key actors in the American economy. They have been and will be the cornerstone of the next safety net.

Mutualist organizations—organizations in which we're meaningfully connected economically and socially with our fellow citizens—are the delivery mechanisms for a better life. They are already the places where we're solving problems in our own communities, and that means they are the base on which tomorrow's social contract will rest. Mutualist organizations routinely engage in sophisticated financial transactions at scale, but having a social purpose remains at the core of their DNA. In the past, they built a national safety net, and today they continue to deliver local safety nets to communities everywhere as well.

Why do we keep looking only to the for-profit sector or government to solve the problem of creating the next safety net? What if, instead of a one-size-fits-all safety net delivered through a government agency, you could instead access a safety net in your own neighborhood? What if from the moment you left your house in the morning, every organization you came into contact with was a mutualist organization? You bought groceries at a local food cooperative, worked in a cooperative co-working space, traded expertise or skills you needed for your work through a mutual aid society that was about professional reciprocity, worshipped at a local religious institution (or communed with brother and sister atheists), and finally picked up your kids from a babysitting cooperative you started with your friends.

Though the mutualist ecosystems workers build for themselves can grow large, they start out small—and are designed to be human-scale at every step. They're diverse, not homogeneous, and getting meaningfully involved with one is always within your reach. A sapling may take a generation to fill out into a tree, but there are roles you can play at every step of its growth. You can be the one to plant the sapling. You can enjoy the shade of the mature tree. Or you can make yourself part of its growth along the way. Whatever role you choose, you'll be joining the mutualist coalition—a coalition built around how you and those you love will meet your needs now and in the future. This kind of worker-built world is not so far-fetched. Mutual ecosystems have existed before, and workers are continuing to build them today.

CHAPTER 4

Mutualist Ecosystems

Building Biodiverse Scale

In 2013, the City of Detroit, Michigan, declared bankruptcy. The U.S. territory of Puerto Rico followed suit a few years later. For years now, Hartford, Connecticut, has been on the brink as well. This was all before COVID-19 hit, sending record numbers of people into unemployment and off the tax rolls that cities rely on to fund themselves. Over the next decade, more and more local and state governments are going to struggle to provide basic services to their citizens, even wealthy cities and states like New York. To people like me, who pay attention to how our communities fund themselves, the future looks bleak if we're going to keep looking to the same binary solution of free markets or government interventions. Local, city, and state governments are in a weaker position to deliver basic services to us than ever before, at the very moment we need them most.

How will we make our communities into places we want to live in again?

We'll have to do it ourselves, by building the institutions

we need. New networks of mutualist organizations are the only way we'll be able to build back the core economic functions of cities: healthcare, schools, job training, access to healthy food. Once we've done that, we'll see how government can support these new institutions, and elect new leaders who are eager to partner with the mutualist sector. But we can't wait to get started.

Citizens should first look for places where mutualism already exists. Are there unions in the community? Is there a food or other kind of cooperative? Are there religious communities that already meet and care for their neighbors? Are there community leaders who know how to connect people? But one or two mutualist institutions in our community won't be enough to build the next safety net. To do that, we'll have to reorient our frame of reference. We'll have to ask ourselves how we can knit these organizations together into something bigger.

But how do we do that? By starting small and solving the problems we encounter in our own lives first. Even the most robust mutualist ecosystems start out with a problem to solve and a community to solve it for, then grow from there.

My family's union, the ILGWU, was part of one such ecosystem. The "needle unions" in New York City in the 1910s and '20s formed a complex network that did more than just bargain for higher wages—though that's how they started. Over time, they became an essential part of their members' day-to-day existence: they funded housing, built health clinics, and helped their members live well-rounded lives.

While the ILGWU played an essential part in that moment in history, the most exemplary mutualist innovation was happening at the other major clothing union, the Amalgamated Clothing Workers of America. That union was led by one of America's most gifted mutualists, Sidney Hillman, an immigrant from Lithuania who started out in the labor movement on the shop floor as a garment cutter.

The Amalgamated Clothing Workers of America was founded in 1914 by a group of men's clothing workers who were dissatisfied with their previous union, the United Garment Workers of America, and its concessions during a strike. They needed a leader, and they found one in Sidney Hillman. When Hillman took the job, he set out to solve the problem that was right in front of him: getting the American Federation of Labor to recognize his Amalgamated union and growing the union's membership. Under Hillman, the Amalgamated quickly found legitimacy among those who mattered: from 1916 to 1919, membership increased from 48,000 to 138,000, and Amalgamated became the fourth-largest industrial union in the United States.

But Hillman was an entrepreneur and an innovator by nature. Not content just to win basic protections for his workers, he set his sights higher: What if Amalgamated could help workers solve other problems in their daily lives? What if, for instance, the union could help members borrow money, buy a house, get healthcare, and receive an education? Hillman wanted to tackle these kinds of problems next, but he needed more than just a union to do it.

Hillman realized he needed patient capital, which then meant he needed a bank. If he wanted to help his workers get better housing and to give those workers more agency in their own lives, they first needed an institution that would loan them money. In an era in which opening a checking account could sometimes require a significant deposit and getting a loan required substantial collateral, there were few financial institutions available for assembly workers. The bank Hillman had in mind, by contrast, would be designed specifically to loan money to people just like his clothing workers.

Amalgamated Bank of New York opened its doors in New York City on April 14, 1923, just off Union Square on East Fourteenth Street. Opening day was a success. J. S. Potofsky, vice president of the Amalgamated union, later wrote that 2,400 workers deposited nearly half a million dollars in the bank within the first few days alone, drawn in by services they couldn't find anywhere else: loans based on no collateral other than a worker's good name; small loans to get workers through short periods of unemployment; low-cost remittances back to a worker's home country; and nonexploitative investment advice and services for smaller investors. The bank made no loans to clothing manufacturers, thereby avoiding a conflict of interest by, as Potofsky put it, "segregating the union from banking operations." Amalgamated Bank hired experts, professors, and bankers who may not otherwise have been sympathetic to union causes but who were likely fascinated by the experiment. The bank put the workers first, limiting the ownership of stock and dividends, which in turn reduced the temptation to prioritize chasing profits over offering services to customers. "In the case of the labor bank," Potofsky said, "the profits are merely the yardstick to denote the successful operation of the bank—a mere byproduct, as it were."

Once the bank was established, Amalgamated's members and Hillman alike had new access to capital. Hillman continued to establish a range of other businesses under the Amalgamated umbrella, each of which existed to allow the members of the Amalgamated Clothing Workers of America to lead richer, fuller lives. By 1926, the list of businesses included Amalgamated Centre, a real estate holding company; ACW Credit Union, a company for extending loans to members that predated the bank; Amalgamated Trust & Savings Bank of Chicago; Russian-American Industrial Corporation, which helped workers make remittances back to their home country (the current president of Amalgamated Bank, Keith Mestrich, told me that Amalgamated pioneered the field of remittances in America); ACW Corporation, a purchasing cooperative; Paramount Holding Corporation, a real estate company that managed the union's real estate holdings; and Amalgamated Investors Inc., "for the purposes of cooperative investment." At its height, the Amalgamated union's membership numbered around 177,000, and these businesses served them all.

Leyla Vural, who worked with me at Working Today and whose PhD dissertation focused on this period of Hillman's life, is one of the only people I know of who has written about Hillman's Amalgamated in detail from a business strategy perspective. By 1927, Hillman was building cooperative housing in the Bronx and on the Lower East Side to, as Leyla puts it, "demonstrate that [Amalgamated] could successfully administer a complex venture." But, as she writes, building housing didn't just require a bank. It also required a law. That law had come in 1926 when the New York State government, facing a housing shortage, offered twenty-year tax exemptions to builders. Amalgamated, she writes, "had waited anxiously for this day, having already selected a piece of land in the Bronx. The [Amalgamated Clothing Workers of America] became the first organization to make use of the new law." This is the role government can play in supporting mutualism: it enabled Amalgamated to grow by passing laws that provided a path to scale.

Ground was broken for the Amalgamated Housing Cooperative on Thanksgiving Day of 1926, on the site that Amalgamated had reserved in the Bronx, next to Van Cortlandt Park. The buildings rose quickly. Amalgamated's union newspaper wrote in 1928, "A thousand gifted orators telling the workers what they could do if they would with their massed money power could not be as convincing as the group of six buildings in the upper Bronx. There stands against a winter skyline a more convincing argument for cooperation than was ever uttered by the most gifted speaker. They are a promise of what all the workers some day will do for themselves."

The new buildings were managed by the Amalgamated Housing Corporation, which, like the bank, existed to serve its members first. Once workers bought into the cooperative, at a cost of $500 per room, they owned a piece of stock in the corporation. Only residents could own stock, preventing outside investors from using the apartments as investment vehicles. After all, profit wasn't the point. As Vural writes, "The Amalgamated Housing Corporation did not pay stock dividends; rather, if there was a surplus, tenant-cooperators received a rent rebate."

Once the buildings were built and occupied, other cooperative ventures began to spring up among their residents. According to Vural, residents started a cooperative summer camp for children; a cooperative daycare; a cooperative grocery store; a library with books in English, Yiddish, and Russian; and educational clubs and activities, including artist workshops, lectures, concerts, and shows. They even bought a block in the Bronx and built a two-hundred-car parking garage on it, with the goal of starting a cooperative shopping center with twenty-two stores.

Hillman died in 1946, but the Amalgamated Clothing Workers of America continued to expand the mission of social unionism. In April of 1951, the first Sidney Hillman Health Clinic opened in New York City. A low-cost specialty clinic designed to give union members access to high-quality care, it scheduled more than 45,000 appointments for workers in its first year. It proved so popular that Amalgamated soon extended healthcare to the wives and children of union members as well. The clinic operated at its original location at 16 East Sixteenth Street until 2017, and it continues to provide care today.

I once asked Sidney Hillman's daughter, Philoine Hillman Fried, how her father decided what new ventures to invest in. She told me that he simply listened to workers and then solved their problems.

At first, I was underwhelmed by her response. But over time I came to realize that this was actually a powerful design strategy for social purpose organizations. The value that these organizations can offer has to come from listening to what people *need*. And the organizations can be viable only if they choose meaningful problems that are actually solvable. Hillman's philosophy wasn't grandiose precisely because he saw that not all problems can be solved and that hard problems can't always be solved first.

Hillman started out by solving the problems that were right in front of him, but over time the Amalgamated union turned into something bigger: the anchor institution in a mutualist ecosystem that included cooperative housing, a shared vacation destination, a health clinic for workers, an insurance company, a bank, and more. Hillman and his staff built a network with leaders pulled from his workforce—lawyers, financiers, real estate developers, and others committed to the union—who helped him identify members' needs and develop a strategy to meet them. This ecosystem was economically interconnected; Hillman would use revenues from one business to provide seed funding for another. But each organization was also its own separate economic entity with its own separate economic mechanism.

Soon, Amalgamated's workers weren't just dues-paying members of a union. They were human beings embedded in a rich network of mutualist institutions that touched their lives in meaningful ways every day, from the doctors who cared for them to the very roofs over their heads. This network collectively addressed the basic needs that all workers share: those for food, shelter, and good health. But it also addressed other needs that workers had then, just as they do today, including a feeling of well-being. Amalgamated recognized that bread alone wasn't enough for its members, but that they were whole human beings with a need for art, culture, and nature: "bread and roses" was the saying. Amalgamated wasn't just a union; it was the bedrock of a network of organizations that formed a remarkably effective and complete safety net. Amalgamated provided its members with a sturdier set of protections than most of us have today.

How can we build a mutualist ecosystem like the one Amalgamated built one hundred years ago, but that addresses the needs of workers today?

The process by which a leader builds a mutualist group is no more complicated than this: Identify your community, talk to them, and *listen* to them. Listen for their problems, and listen especially for the problems that are solvable. Then start solving. This is the way every mutualist ecosystem I've ever encountered starts out, and that includes the mutualist ecosystem that I started myself: the Freelancers Union.

Like Sidney Hillman, I didn't set out to start an ecosystem. Also like him, I was just trying to solve a problem—specifically, the one I encountered in my own life when I started out as a lawyer.

It was 1994. I was furious that the law firm I'd just joined was planning to categorize me and a few colleagues as "independent contractors." The now familiar gig economy notion of misclassification—for example, the Uber driver who relies entirely on Uber for her livelihood and yet is not considered to be an employee of Uber, thus leaving her ineligible for common labor protections—was new even for union lawyers like us. But we did recognize that there were two tiers of lawyers at our firm, and that we were the ones worse off. We weren't eligible for health insurance or a pension. We weren't eligible for unemployment insurance or protected by gender discrimination laws. We didn't get paid sick days, personal days, vacation days, or holidays. Our gallows-humor joke— that we should call ourselves the Transient Workers Union, motto "The Union Makes Us . . . Not So Weak"—got to the heart of our predicament. As independent contractors, we were not, by definition of the National Labor Relations Act, protected if we formed or joined a union. A union of freelancers was a contradiction in terms.

It's ironic that I started to think seriously about the future of work as a result of getting screwed by a progressive labor law firm. But now I had a new frame by which to analyze the world, and I became my own laboratory. It was already clear to me that we were heading toward a two-tier economy, with traditional workers on one track and the growing independent workforce on the other. This new type of freelancer was funding their own health insurance, retirement, even paid time off, themselves. Employers' growing reliance on temporary workers, combined with changes in technology that made it easier to rely on a fleet of remote contractors, meant that a new class of workers was emerging. It cut across ages, demographics, and socioeconomic lines—a generation of freelancers and part-time workers with short-term jobs whose relationship to employment was fundamentally different from that of their parents. I would have missed it entirely if I hadn't become one of them.

This feeling of isolation was new to me. I grew up in the 1970s. We were a deeply interconnected family: my grandfather Israel and his mother, the first Sara Horowitz, had started the Horowitz Cousins Club when they arrived in New York, a dues-paying association exclusively for our family, with a president, a vice president (my father), and a secretary-treasurer (the only woman). In my father's generation, there were eight cousins who planned annual get-togethers, the most important of which was the annual Passover seder. More than forty people would attend, and we'd use the money from dues to rent a catering hall. When I was six, my cousin Diane, who was twelve at the time, sat next to me as I tried to read my paragraph from the Haggadah for the first time. We sat at basic folding tables with tablecloths and endless relatives, some of them first-generation immigrants, whose names I could never remember. But I felt like I was part of a big family, and I could see in the Yiddish culture, humor, and food that I was part of a tradition that was bigger than I was. Today, I still go to Diane's house every year at Passover, where Diane, my cousin David, my sister, Anne, and I are the four from the original Horowitz clan who along with the next generation keep the Cousins Club alive.

It was such a different time, when new social movements were a huge part of American life. My mother was the breadwinner in our family, and she sent me to a Quaker school, which in many ways embodied the spirit of the era. The headmaster of the lower school, John Darr, was a minister and peace activist. I remember only that he seemed very tall and preternaturally kind, but I later learned that he stood up to the House Un-American Activities Committee and refused to name names during the McCarthy era.

As in all Quaker schools, we had a morning assembly that began with a few minutes of silence. One day when I was about nine, we had a special guest. I remember that I was sitting on a pew-like bench on the left side of the auditorium at the Brooklyn Friends School at 375 Pearl Street when an older Black man took the stage next to Mr. Darr. He told us that his name was Bayard Rustin, that he was a Quaker himself, and that he had come to talk to us about the civil rights movement. We learned that he had helped organize the March on Washington for Jobs and Freedom a decade before, and though I was too young then to remember anything specific that he said, I do remember that his independence and his sense of a true north about his beliefs struck me deeply. I loved listening to him talk about how he had committed himself to the labor movement at an early age. A decade later, at the age of eighteen, I made the decision to do the same. I enrolled at the Cornell University School of Industrial and Labor Relations and have been part of the labor movement ever since.

By 1994, I was in my thirties, and I was trying to figure out what a commitment to labor looked like in a changing economy. Because work was becoming so episodic, protections needed to follow workers from job to job and project to project, not just attach to employees who worked for a single company. The new economy called for a whole new legal and regulatory process that accepted and supported the new ways that people worked.

But it was the mid-nineties, and by then the post-Reagan worldview felt like an unstoppable wave. The Democratic Party and the progressive community had internalized the call for a smaller government, and as a result had shifted their attention to focusing only on vulnerable workers. But this new frame of reference meant that when I talked with foundations about the need for a new safety net for freelancers who earned, say, $50,000 a year, I was told that those workers were "rich" and didn't need any help. At first, I thought I might be missing something. My math put $50,000 a year firmly in the working class. But now I realize that instead of engaging with Reaganism's assault on the working class at its roots, Democrats were in a defensive crouch just trying to survive Reaganism. As a result, no one was even articulating the need for new kinds of protections for this new working class, let alone building the institutions that could deliver them. This new workforce needed a new kind of union to listen to what they needed and to solve problems on their behalf.

But what would that new union look like?

The new union would have to grapple with the fact that

the most exposed workers were independent contractors, who have no protections to form or join a union under the Wagner Act. The new union would have to be a union of freelancers, even though this was a contradiction in terms. I grew up in a dedicated labor family, and my mother taught me to believe that not only could I achieve anything but also that I had an obligation to try.

Not quite sure how I was going to build a new kind of unionism but sure that I had to, I left the law firm and enrolled at the Kennedy School of Government at Harvard, treating it as a kind of intellectual sabbatical. Ten days in, I read a column in *The New York Times* describing the Columbia University sociologist Herbert Gans and his idea for a jobs lobby. This fit my intuition: we needed to have a discussion about work that was about *all* workers, including independent contractors, not just those working conventional forty-hour weeks. It's funny: the lowest grade I got at the Kennedy School was in Introduction to Labor, Health, and Education Policy. They kept teaching that when there's a social problem, the best thing to do is to start a social program to fix it. I kept thinking, *If there's a social problem, organize the community to solve it.* The truth is, I've been having that same argument ever since.

What I loved about the Kennedy School was that you had to argue your point. It forced me to be really honest with myself about what I believed and what organizing strategies could actually work. It was a difficult time for me. Being committed to what I thought was necessary to build the next form of unionism required me to break away with some key views of the current left, which at the time felt two-dimensional and not as pro-union as I was. I rejected categorically the idea that progressives should focus on only one half of the working class. I finished the Kennedy School's two-year program in one year and in 1995 founded Working Today, the nonprofit that would become the Freelancers Union in 2001.

The year I started Working Today, Bob Herbert wrote a great piece about us for *The New York Times* titled "Strength in Numbers." The idea that this new workforce of freelancers could organize was so powerful that people started sending checks to our nascent organization and asking for meetings. Working Today was a kind of advocacy innovation lab, where we developed a policy agenda that would not only help freelancers but also educate policy makers, elected officials, foundations, and think tanks about the changes coming to the workforce. I realized that we were doing what Sidney Hillman had always done: we were listening to workers and trying to solve their problems.

I spent a lot of time with freelancers and listened to what they told me. Their biggest challenge was access to affordable, quality health insurance, and though insurance wasn't a particularly exciting proposition (or something I thought I could fix quickly), I realized that solving the insurance problem could directly address a fundamental existential uncertainty that most freelancers face: When the worst happens, will they be prepared for it? Even the most successful freelancers feel a gnawing in their gut when considering that question.

I took it upon myself to learn everything I could about the insurance industry. I learned that the twentieth-century paradigm most of us were familiar with, built during the manufacturing era when most workers had traditional jobs with big companies, was useless for freelancers. I learned that most insurance companies were focused on short-term profits rather than the health of their customers. I learned that there were only three categories of health insurance markets in America—individual, small group (for small business), and large group (for big corporations)—and that freelancers, who were in the individual market, had access to the worst care at the highest prices and by definition couldn't qualify for the other two markets.

We put a provision into our earliest 501(c)(3) nonprofit filing for Working Today saying that we would be providing insurance to model a new kind of portable benefits system, and we eventually settled on a brokerage model. We'd negotiate to get freelancers to be recognized as a group and act as an intermediary, selling insurance to them at a lower rate than they could find elsewhere. Brokering insurance is a tried-and-true business model, but in our case we weren't trying to make money from it. Instead, we were using it as an economic mechanism to fund our nonprofit. Since brokerages are required by regulators to be for-profit businesses, we created a new insurance brokerage business just to serve freelancers. It was a for-profit, wholly owned by the nonprofit, ensuring that no money left our little ecosystem. We could build out revenue through the brokerage and recycle it back into Working Today to continue our advocacy work.

Mixing union advocacy and benefits made sense: we knew our community well and could make their insurance go further. We kept asking our members which caregivers they recommended and created our own internal freelancers' mini-network of the best, most affordable providers. We were a bunch of liberal arts majors providing insurance, but it turned out that we were in a good position to be doing so. By now it was 1997, twenty years before today's data wars, but friends in the burgeoning New York tech scene had the foresight to tell me how essential it was that I negotiate for our data with every insurance company I entered into business with. We were amassing a wealth of information about who our members were and what they were looking for in an insurance product, and soon this information would come in handy.

Around this time, people started to notice what I was up to. In 1999, the MacArthur Foundation awarded me one of their "genius grant" fellowships, calling me "a pioneer in shaping institutions and services for a changing workforce in America." The fellowship was a good opportunity for us at Working Today to step back and think expansively. If we had no financial constraints, how far would our imaginations stretch? I remember standing at the whiteboard working through the numbers of what we would do if we had, say, $25 million. As soon as we asked the question, the answer was obvious: with that kind of money, we would start an insurance company. Not a brokerage, but a real insurance company that could build health plans specifically tuned to the needs of freelancers.

It was a crazy idea, but it stuck. After all, offering specialized health insurance packages has always been an essential part of what unions do, and this kind of specialization is why union members often prefer their private health insurance plans over nationalized insurance strategies. We could offer care that met freelancers where they lived, making sure things like anxiety, depression, carpal tunnel syndrome, and other afflictions common to freelance workers were covered. Luckily, we had data about exactly what those afflictions were and what they cost. In the mid-2000s, our actuary looked at the profile of our now four-thousand-strong membership base, did the math, and came up with an economic model that worked. We could build a self-sustaining, freelancer-focused insurance company if we had some startup capital to fund our reserves. We needed $17 million, to be exact. The idea of the Freelancers Insurance Company was born.

It was a lot of money, but because we already had a solid revenue model through our brokerage, we were able to qualify for some of the best forms of long-term investment offered by the foundation world. In 2000, the Ford Foundation gave us $1 million worth of loans and $600,000 worth of grants for our experiment in starting the first portable benefits network. From there, we were able to go back to investors and look for the rest of the money we needed to get off the ground. In the end, we managed to raise $10 million in loans and an additional $7 million in grants: $17 million.

We were able to raise this money because we were lucky that a few smart people at the foundations we worked with also understood the power of Sidney Hillman's mutualist design strategy: start with the problems you can solve. If we started a portable benefits model with workers who could afford to buy the insurance, we could demonstrate that the model could work on a larger scale. We could then extrapolate and cover lower-wage workers as well, paying for it with the revenues from the more highly paid freelancers. And that's just what we did.

We got so much wrong in our first year that we almost went out of business. But even though most of us lacked a formal background in insurance, we were problem solvers and got good advice from veteran insurance people who were part of our senior team. We quickly began to see where our organization was bleeding: our expenses were huge, we were not managing our costs, and we were forced to make difficult decisions about what kinds of medical issues we could realistically cover without going out of business. So we started to look for solutions.

We tried to view our biggest spends as opportunities to serve our members rather than as cost centers that needed to be contained. After all, we weren't in this to make money for ourselves. For example, we knew that anxiety and carpal tunnel syndrome were going to be enormous spends for our population, but we also knew that freelancers needed this kind of care more than anything. Similarly, triplets and premature babies are hugely expensive for insurance companies, but we wanted to make sure that freelancers who were also mothers were protected. So we doubled down and actually became *more* involved in our members' care. By talking to them, helping to coordinate their care, and evaluating their progress, we managed to become partners with them while also containing our own costs. This is something many really good insurance companies do, and we were able to align our members' needs with an economic model that worked. By the second year, we started breaking even. Soon after that, we became profitable, and for three straight years we did not raise premiums.

This is how I know that mutualist organizations can deliver the next safety net. I know it because we did it. Workers felt better getting their benefits from an institution they felt connected to. Those were wonderful years, and I was leading one of the most committed staffs I've ever worked with: talented people who put problem solving and building first; seasoned insurance executives who wanted us to succeed; a brilliant chief technology officer, Ohad Folman, who built our tech stack from scratch; and the ingenious Ann Boger, who built the operational infrastructure and who has been a fifteen-year partner to me in insurance innovation.

But we realized we could still be better and smarter. So a small group of us, the key employees of what was now called the Freelancers Union, got on a plane and flew to Emilia-Romagna, a region in Italy near Bologna, where two out of three citizens are members of some kind of cooperative. A few years later, I visited the Basque region of Spain, where an ecosystem of cooperatives under the umbrella of the Mondragon Corporation, which had been an inspiration of mine for years, had transformed the economy of the region. People in both places had been practicing a mature, sophisticated kind of mutualism far longer than we had, and I wanted to learn from the best.

First, Mondragon. The Mondragon Corporation, the largest worker cooperative in the world, is actually a federation of hundreds of smaller cooperatives, all based near the village of Mondragon, in the Mondragon Valley of Spain. Founded in 1956, Mondragon traces its roots to 1941, when a Catholic priest, José María Arizmendiarrieta, nicknamed "Arizmendi," arrived in the Mondragon Valley to preach, only to find a region that had been devastated socially and economically by the recent civil war.

While I was there, I met with Mondragon's ambassador to North America, a man named Michael Peck. Peck recently told me that Arizmendi didn't go to Mondragon to build a multinational cooperative corporation. But when he saw the devastation of the Mondragon Valley, he had no choice but to act. "They say that necessity is the mother of invention," Peck said. "When you're in front of the horror show, you quickly innovate because you know that dealing with the horror is no longer an option. . . . People had to eat;

they had to face the winters." Arizmendi met with suspicion at first. "He couldn't get people to come together, so he organized soccer matches, football matches, people playing sports and cooperating," Peck told me.

When a culture of collaboration began to sink in, Arizmendi took the next step. He set up a technical school that enrolled the town's young people, with the goal of teaching them skills they could apply to manufacturing jobs. Years later, in 1956, five of his graduates returned to the Mondragon Valley and joined with him to start a worker cooperative called Ulgor, an initialism of the first letter of each of the five co-founders' last names. Ulgor manufactured paraffin burners, and was so successful that other local businesses began to imitate not only the company's success but also the Christian humanism that Arizmendi preached and that was at Ulgor's core. The ecosystem of cooperatives that became Mondragon was born.

"He found his life's mission," Peck told me of Arizmendi, but "it took him fifteen years, and that's something people don't really appreciate. People, especially in America, want to add water and stir and get instant results. But building an ecosystem from the ground up takes time. You have to get the culture and you have to get the thinking and the vocabulary right, and it took this priest fifteen years."

In 1959, Arizmendi convinced his fellow workers to start cooperative banking and insurance businesses: Caja Laboral Popular, a bank that could fund the cooperative enterprises, and Lagun Aro, a welfare system. Like Sidney Hillman, Arizmendi recognized that addressing some of the workers' most basic needs—access to money and to a social security system of benefits—was the first step toward helping them lead richer lives.

The Mondragon ethic is simple and rooted in the Rochdale Principles: every worker gets a vote; management will never make more than eight times what the lowest-paid worker on the factory floor makes; education is crucial; and cooperatives should learn to work cooperatively with other cooperatives. The technical school that Arizmendi founded was eventually formalized as Mondragon University, and the bank, school, and welfare system became resources that worker-owned cooperatives in the region came to rely on as they continued to expand the Mondragon business ethic. As the network of cooperatives grew, each set aside about 70 percent of its profits for redistribution to cooperatives that were underperforming. Today, Mondragon is the largest worker-owned cooperative in the world, taking in more than $13.5 billion in revenue annually and employing over seventy thousand employees. What's more, it has made the Basque region remarkably prosperous. A former Mondragon executive once put it this way: "If the Basque region in Spain were a country, it would have the second-lowest income inequality in the world."

Which is not to say that Mondragon hasn't weathered its share of challenges. In the aftermath of the financial crisis of 2007–2008, Mondragon's very first cooperative, the paraffin burner manufacturer Ulgor (which had been renamed Fagor in the 1980s), began to fail, and in 2013 Mondragon made the unprecedented decision to cut off support for it, the first time Mondragon had allowed one of its cooperatives to fail. Peck told me that Mondragon received plenty of criticism over this move from those on the left and right alike, who saw it as evidence that the entire Mondragon system had failed. But, as Peck told me, "Fagor had a forty-to-forty-five-year run, much longer than most of the companies on the stock exchanges." And what Mondragon did with that failure is actually evidence of just how robust a mutualist ecosystem Mondragon really is. Rather than lay off Fagor's employees, Mondragon was able to support them with benefits through Lagun Aro, retrain them at Mondragon University, and ultimately find many of them new positions. Fifteen hundred out of the eighteen hundred laid-off Fagor workers found placement in other Mondragon cooperatives within the year. Mondragon has been successful and capable of resilience in the face of crises precisely because it approaches cooperative economics as an ecosystem. It has a philosophy that scale is good, because scale helps its worker-owners compete on the international stage.

I asked Peck what he thought Arizmendi's North Star was. "His North Star was that it's all about quality and dignified employment . . . ," Peck said. "Everything was built around the human as the most valued resource."

Mondragon is a unique organization, the only one of its kind in the world. Its origins are unique, too, and Peck told me that there is no magic formula to create a new Mondragon. But there are a few lessons we can learn from its success. First, Mondragon wouldn't have been possible if the local government hadn't recognized that something special was happening in the Mondragon Valley and taken steps to advocate for it with the Spanish government in Madrid. "Mondragon depends on Basque regional governments in the three provinces to defend its cooperative status to the central government in Madrid," Peck told me, "whether it's to socialists or to the right of center, neither of whom have good feelings about cooperatives." Mondragon requires skilled advocates who understand its model and are able to lobby for support from the national government.

But perhaps more important, Mondragon teaches us that so much more can be done with a national government that really understands cooperatives. "There's an incredible commercial movement," Peck told me, "which is hanging by invisible legislative threads. There's no strong governmental legislative support for this stuff anywhere, and [Mondragon] managed to survive without it." If an ecosystem like Mondragon can thrive in spite of the fact that the Spanish government's support for it is only glancing, what could it do with a government that really understood what it was trying to accomplish? I've often asked myself this in regard to the United States. Peck agrees: "Think of what we could do if there was an actual mandate for something."

When my team and I visited the Emilia-Romagna region in northern Italy, near the city of Bologna, just before we launched the Freelancers Insurance Company, a mandate for mutualism was just what we found. The cooperativism there is something you have to see to understand: a decentralized local cooperative economy built from the ground up that nonetheless participates in global markets. In a region of only 4 million people, there are somewhere between 7,500 and 15,000 co-ops accounting for over one-third of the region's GDP. Two-thirds of the citizens in the region are members of a co-op.

The result is that Emilia-Romagna has one of the most equitable distributions of income in the world, making for a rich, egalitarian, interconnected society in which cooperativism is an integral part of everyday life: retail cooperatives; construction cooperatives; agricultural cooperatives; cooperative housing; and cooperative manufacturing, from small-scale (woodworking and cabinetry cooperatives in Tuscany) to large (construction for large-scale public works projects). But even more important are the cooperatives that occupy the social services sector, an especially robust part of the cooperative economy in Italy: cooperative healthcare, elder care, and care for the disabled. It's no accident that the Emilia-Romagna approach to education—a student-focused, student-directed model that stresses the value of the community in raising a child—came out of this region as well.

I love Emilia-Romagna. Its rich history and culture make life there wonderful. I've been there three times now, and each time I go, I can't stop eating its great, affordable food. In America, eating well is a privilege. In Emilia-Romagna, it's a way of life.

When my team first visited the region, we were shown around by Matt Hancock, an American who had studied in Emilia-Romagna and become an expert on the region's cooperative economy. He told us that the region's intricate network of cooperatives was the product in large part of the Italian communists and partisans who fought hard against the Nazis and Italian fascism in World War II. After the war, those who survived rebuilt. "The people who came back from the hills [after] fighting the Nazis were the people who were the first mayors in postwar Emilia-Romagna," Hancock told me. "They were the leaders of the labor unions. They started co-ops or went back into the co-ops that had been in existence prewar. Talk about swords into plowshares: quite literally, the resistance fighters laid down their arms and built the society they'd been fighting for. . . . People made huge sacrifices because they really did believe they were doing something now that they would never see but their kids and their grandkids would be living. . . . I think it had an almost religious kind of fervor to it. You know: faith."

In 1948, those values and that faith were written into Article 45 of Italy's new constitution. In the words of Vera Zamagni, a professor of economics at the University of Bologna who has studied Italy's unusual cooperative economic structure, this new constitution "recognized the interest of the nation in the promotion of cooperation as a way of keeping together economic activity and solidaristic motivations." In other words, the Italian government wrote mutualism into the country's constitution, and in the process both defined and protected the concept for future generations.

New laws over the following decades built on this strong foundation, and in the 1970s and '80s these laws created capital structures that we simply don't have in the United States. A 1977 law, for example, exempted "indivisible reserves," or undistributed profits set aside to be reinvested in cooperativism, from corporate taxation. In 1983, a law was passed allowing a cooperative to own or hold a majority stake in a for-profit capitalist business or corporation. And a 1992 law requires cooperatives to put 3 percent of their profits into a fund that goes toward capitalizing and promoting the creation of new cooperative enterprises—in other words, the law requires and incentivizes cooperatives to replicate themselves.

These funds are managed by experts—experts who in any other context would be called venture capitalists. But these are venture capitalists of the cooperative world, who have to make decisions about where funding will go based on which enterprises have the greatest chances of success. They are doing this within a local, deeply interconnected ecosystem and are concerned first and foremost with making sure there is high employment in the region rather than seeking a return on investment. These cooperative venture capitalists have very strict rules about investment; after all, to maintain high levels of employment, businesses in the region have to be really good businesses.

During our visit, I met with representatives from the oldest—and, according to Hancock, the biggest—federation of cooperatives in the region: Legacoop, which traces its origins back to the late nineteenth century. These men applied the same skill set as venture capitalists in America, but to a different metric: making sure that the citizens of Emilia-Romagna had good jobs. Just as with Sidney Hillman's Amalgamated Bank, for them profits were just a by-product of success.

The dense ecosystem of cooperativism in Emilia-Romagna arose organically. Although the original anchors were the communists, partisans, and faith-based groups that wanted to rebuild their communitarian way of life after the war, today the region has no umbrella organization, no president, no official coordination. It thrives because of the reciprocal obligations among co-ops and among the citizens, for whom co-ops are an important part of their daily lives. This culture of building is perpetuated by the core mutualist values of these institutions, passed on from generation to generation, so that it is now encoded in the DNA of the communities. Not only is Emilia-Romagna an ecosystem in the most organic sense of the word, started by a community of people for their own sake, but it also exists in a region where the government has written a mandate for cooperatives into law. It is one of the best examples of what an activist government, one that evolves and grows in tandem with global changes while staying embedded in a philosophy of mutualism, can accomplish.

What could happen with a similar mandate in America?

. . .

We came back to New York with an entirely different perspective on what we were building. We weren't just creating an affordable insurance alternative for freelancers or a new form of unionism. We were laying the groundwork for a mutualist ecosystem, a complex web of economically connected mutualist organizations that all ran independently of one another but that all existed to serve one community. The Freelancers Union was the anchor, the epicenter of our freelancer community, and we had already built the Freelancers Union brokerage and the Freelancers Insurance Company. But as we listened more closely to our community, we began to collectively envision a larger ecosystem. It was an inchoate vision at first, and the Freelancers Union was certainly no Mondragon or Emilia-Romagna—yet. But maybe we could show that there was no reason something similar couldn't happen in America, too, someday.

Once I started to listen closely to the workers who used our insurance, I realized that what freelancers really wanted was somewhere to go to receive their medical care that was geared toward their needs. Our insurance was great, but they cared more about health in the holistic sense of *wellness*. They cared about quality food, alternative medicine, acupuncture, and mental health, and they wanted a healthcare provider who understood that about them. Since their work was episodic, since they didn't have sick days and couldn't collect unemployment, they knew they had to take good care of themselves so that they could return to work quickly. But they also wanted a fundamental change in healthcare that was centered on them and the way they led their lives. We came to call this the desire to lead a "360-degree life." What freelancers wanted most of all was to have a sense of control over their time, to care for themselves and for others, and to lead lives that felt fundamentally human.

How could we translate that desire into actionable solutions? I remembered Sidney Hillman's Amalgamated Clothing Workers of America and its incredible healthcare clinic in Manhattan that was just for members of the union. We analyzed the feasibility of a center like that for ourselves and realized we had enough money coming in from our insurance company that we could open one. We looked at successful ecosystems like unionized culinary workers in Atlantic City who had created exactly this kind of center for their members. Following in these past experiments' footsteps, in 2012 we built a medical practice in downtown Brooklyn and hired the best doctor-innovators to build out the patient-centered practice. It was a medical practice with a culture attuned to the way freelancers live and work: a medical center just for freelancers. Our members received vaccines, screenings, and primary care for free, but we also made sure to include a community room with beautiful natural light and the buildings' original windows, where yoga classes, acupuncture treatments, receptions, focus groups, and meetings could take place.

Over the next several years, we continued to build our ecosystem. The whole idea of the Freelancers Union was to create a network that anyone who was a freelancer could join, but unlike a manufacturing-era union, which was usually centered on a local organization in a specific region, our freelancers were all over the country. By 2013, we had around 200,000 members. How could we expand our ecosystem beyond New York to reach all of them? We had been doing educational seminars about topics we knew were important to freelancers: how to create a contract, how to negotiate the right rates, and tips on taxes, for instance. I had been reading about Visa founder Dee Hock's idea of "chaordic structure." "Chaordic" is a neologism that combines the words "chaos" and "order." Hock uses the term to refer to organizations that are deliberately decentralized. To create such an organization, you identify leaders in local communities and give them a task. Out of the decentralized chaos that ensues, order emerges. We tried it ourselves. We gave leaders in communities all over the United States the task of teaching a local group the same curriculum we were teaching in New York. We called these local events Spark, which Caitlin Pearce, our head of advocacy, built into a national program. They form an essential part of the Freelancers Union ecosystem in cities all across America today.

But there was still more to our ecosystem. When we founded the Freelancers Insurance Company, it was before services like Stripe existed to make it easy to render payments to and receive payments from huge numbers of people. So we formed a for-profit subsidiary called Independent Worker Solutions and pioneered a new type of group infrastructure where we took thousands of individual payments from freelancers and bundled them to send to dozens of service providers. We were one of the earliest insurtech (combining technology with insurance for innovation and efficiency) startups. I was the CEO and Ann Boger was the COO—two female tech founders in the mid-2000s—with technology built and maintained by Ohad Folman and, later, our staff. Eventually, we spun this company off so its employees could take it over. Today, this by-product of our mutualist ecosystem is a successful tech company in its own right, Zipari.

By about 2004, our ecosystem model had become self-sustaining: we offered services to a community of freelancers that funded our ability to create new and better services for that community and to craft an advocacy agenda that would have a real impact on their lives. Our first step had been to get our economic house in order and to listen to our members' most urgent needs. Now that we had earned the trust of freelancers by doing that, we could begin to lobby local government for real change. The revenues from our ecosystem allowed us to mobilize our members to solve one of freelancers' biggest problems: not getting paid. Negotiating with a client who refuses to pay is usually the job of freelancers themselves. Most freelancers can't afford to hire a lawyer, and most lawyers aren't that interested in chasing small payments for cash-poor freelancers. As a result, most freelancers are out of luck.

With a group of labor lawyers, the Freelancers Union staff, and board member Hanan Kolko, we brainstormed policy solutions and came up with a recommendation that we took to the New York City Council: take the burden of proof off the freelancer and put it on the employer. We wanted to require an employer to do something to rebut a claim of nonpayment made by a freelancer, usually by opening up their wallet to hire a lawyer. This would have two effects: First, it would incentivize the employer to simply pay the freelancer to make the claim go away. Second, it would entitle the freelancer to recover double damages and attorney's fees, incentivizing them to make the claim in the first place. Though it might not be worth it for a freelancer to pay a lawyer out of pocket to recover a $2,000 payment, it might be a different story if they stood to make $4,000, plus have their lawyer's fees paid for.

Today, the Freelance Isn't Free Act, which was finally passed in 2016 and took effect in 2017, gives New York City freelancers a level of confidence that they'll get paid for their work. But it never would have passed if we hadn't been able to fund our lobbying efforts and advocacy through the revenues we were bringing in from the insurance company. Mutualists became coalition partners, including Randi Weingarten from the American Federation of Teachers; Make the Road, the largest immigrant-led grassroots organization in New York; and the late labor leader Héctor Figueroa from the 32BJ of the Service Employees International Union (SEIU). They energetically urged Mayor Bill de Blasio and the city council members to support the Freelance Isn't Free Act. The bill ultimately passed the city council unanimously, supported by Republicans and Democrats alike.

Today, mutualist ecosystems are rare and fragile. They're like UNESCO World Heritage sites: unique, idiosyncratic phenomena that are hard to create but easy to destroy. Some, like the AFL-CIO or Mondragon, last for decades. Some, like the Dutch *waterschappen,* last for centuries. But some last for only a few short years. As in nature, these ecosystems can be strong, resilient, and fragile all at the same time.

The difference between ecosystems that last and those that don't often comes down to this: Does government support them? Or does it replace and destroy them?

Building the next safety net will require us to shift our cultural frame away from an expectation that government or markets will continue to be in a position to solve all our problems for us. Instead, workers must begin to build their own

solutions to these problems and to charge their elected officials with recognizing and protecting those new solutions.
After all, *we* know the problems that need to be solved in our
own lives better than anyone.

The most successful mutualist ecosystems have been
scaled, biodiverse networks big enough to build a groundswell of organizational and popular support for their agen-
das until government can no longer afford to ignore them
and must instead recognize them for what they are, protect
them, propel them, and let them grow. This is exactly what
happened in both the labor and civil rights movements of
the twentieth century. But even those seismic social movements started modestly, with workers solving problems in
their own lives.

Because it turns out that solving problems—even the
smallest, most trivial-seeming problems—is exactly how the
most profound social change begins.

CHAPTER 5

Mutualist Transformation

Randolph and Rustin, Building Mutualist Bridges

On September 6, 1963, *Life* magazine ran a cover story on the March on Washington for Jobs and Freedom, which had taken place in Washington, D.C., the previous week. A quarter of a million people had gathered on the National Mall for a daylong program of speakers and music that had culminated in an impassioned speech—remembered today as the "I Have a Dream" speech—by the president of the Southern Christian Leadership Conference, Martin Luther King, Jr. But it wasn't King who was featured on the cover of *Life*. Instead, the cover shows two men in suits, standing in front of the Lincoln Memorial, a set of maps in hand and their eyes fixed on something in the middle distance. As both men gaze into the distance, the photo captures their shared vision of the future. Next to them is a small caption that indicates who they are: "The Leaders: Randolph and Rustin."

These men's names, A. Philip Randolph and Bayard Rustin, are probably unrecognizable to most Americans today. I might not have known about them myself if Rustin hadn't come to my Quaker school when I was a girl and talked to us about civil rights. But years later, when I started the Freelancers Union, I looked to them as models for how to bring together movements to form a coalition with the power to make change.

Their story remains the high-water mark of mutualist cooperation in America. It both rested on and brought together centuries of disparate strands of mutualist organizing, from the cooperative movements of Black workers dating to the eighteenth century, to the early infrastructure built by Black churches in the nineteenth century, to the Black labor movement of the early twentieth century. They came together in a march that, like Gandhi's Salt March in India in 1930, was also a metaphor that transformed our country.

Randolph and Rustin's story is a lesson in perseverance. Their cooperation didn't happen overnight. These two leaders worked tirelessly for decades to get the movements they were rooted in, movements that stretched back hundreds of years, to align. Randolph was raised in the African Methodist Episcopal (AME) Church and came to civil rights through the labor movement. It was due to his efforts more than anyone else's that the labor movement was first integrated in the 1930s (more on that later). During World War II, he worked to integrate the armed forces as well, with help from Rustin. Rustin grew up a Quaker, was educated in the AME Church, and brought a commitment to Gandhi's philosophy of nonviolence to the civil rights movement. Profound change can take decades, and these two men had the wisdom of patience.

The movements we will need tomorrow will be built on

those who came before us, too. The civil rights movement and its symbolic apotheosis, the March on Washington, are among the most exquisite examples of long-term mutualist cooperation in American history—built on an ecosystem of mutualist organizing that didn't start with Randolph and Rustin, but rather was centuries in the making.

The AME Church—in which Randolph was raised and Rustin was educated, and which has been a powerful force for Black self-determination since its founding more than two hundred years ago—traces its roots back to one of the very first Black mutual aid societies in America, the Free African Society.

Absalom Jones and Richard Allen, the two ministers who started the Free African Society in Philadelphia in 1787, started out focused on solving a social problem: people in their community needed a place to worship. Black churchgoers were being physically pulled off their knees during prayer at St. George's, a Philadelphia United Methodist church, and forced to sit in separate galleries in the back. Though the Free African Society started as a mutual aid society, it also gave Jones and Allen the membership base and economic tools they needed to establish churches of their own, in which Black congregants could worship freely. Jones established the first Black Episcopal church in America, the African Episcopal Church of St. Thomas, and Allen founded what would become one of the largest and most influential Black institutions in the United States, the AME Church.

It took some time for Allen to get the AME Church off the ground—he had to sue before the Pennsylvania courts would recognize its legitimacy—but by the early nineteenth century, his new church had a large, active, and growing membership. Congregations of the AME Church soon sprang up everywhere, moving from Philadelphia to New York, Baltimore, Boston, Chicago, Cincinnati, Detroit, Pittsburgh, Washington, and eventually even the antebellum South. By 1856, it had expanded into Haiti and Canada and its members numbered as many as twenty thousand. That same year, the church started Wilberforce University, the first Black-owned-and-operated college, which years later Bayard Rustin would attend. Today, the AME Church is still a powerful force worldwide.

From the beginning, the AME Church was a mutualist anchor for the Black community. During and after slavery, the church took public stands against repatriation to Africa and helped its members achieve stability and independence. According to historian Clarence Walker, it worked with its members to help them "lead purposeful lives, to acquire property, to educate their children, and to be responsible citizens in the communities where they lived." It also served as an incubator of new leaders. Walker notes that leadership positions in the church became a kind of jumping-off point for Blacks who wanted to become politically active. Randolph's father was one minister who followed this path. Although Randolph didn't follow his father into the clergy, the AME Church nonetheless had a formative effect on his ethics.

The AME Church wasn't the only mutualist institution to arise out of early Black mutual cooperation. The Free African Society also prefigured a remarkably diverse ecosystem of Black mutual aid societies in America that helped freed and freeborn Blacks care for their sick, bury their dead, and provide homes for children and the elderly from the eighteenth through the twentieth century.

In the 2014 book *Collective Courage,* political economist Jessica Gordon Nembhard uncovered a remarkably detailed history of Black mutualist activity in America, a history that she says often goes unacknowledged. "In every period of American history African Americans pooled resources to solve personal, family, political, and economic challenges," she writes. "They often addressed freedom, health, child development, education, burial, employment, and investment in cooperative ventures in ways that leveraged and maximized returns and reduced risks." Before emancipation, such cooperative economics happened informally. An enslaved person who managed to buy their own freedom might pool their resources with others to buy another family member—a mother, sister, or brother—out of slavery as well. Later, this cooperative action became widespread. Gordon Nembhard describes how the resulting mutual aid societies worked:

> A group of people who know each other through their neighborhood or church or other organization join an organization to provide a service or set of services. They agree to pay an initial fee to join and a weekly or monthly fee to keep the common fund operating. A specified portion is paid to any member who needs the service, whether he or she is sick and needs a doctor, hospitalization, an income while convalescing, or needs to be buried or needs food or clothing. Sometimes other members donate their services instead of, or in addition to, funds from the organization's treasury. Some societies hire their own doctor or nurse to attend

to members' health needs. . . . These societies paid death benefits of between $10 and $20 and sick benefits from $1 to $3, each on premiums of 25 cents on average. . . . Many families belonged to two or more aid societies in order to increase their sick benefits.

Members of a society would put in a certain amount of money every month or year, and whenever a need came up—someone's mother got sick, or someone was hurt and unable to work—that member would be able to take money out of the collective pot to defray the expense.

Over time, these early mutual aid societies became more sophisticated and grew into Black schools, insurance companies, credit associations and banks, and other cooperative organizations. There was a Black cooperative shipyard, the Chesapeake Marine Railway and Dry Dock Company, in Baltimore. There were Black cooperative associations of farmers in the freed South after the Civil War. In the early twentieth century, W.E.B. Du Bois saw the importance of cooperativism to the Black community, believing that cooperatives would, as Gordon Nembhard writes, "provide the economic opportunities denied to African Americans and would allow Blacks to serve the common good rather than be slaves to market forces." Gordon Nembhard posits that Du Bois saw even the Underground Railroad as a kind of cooperative—an example, as she puts it, of "high-level social and economic cooperation and collaboration among African Americans and between Blacks and Whites."

But Randolph recognized that in the industrial era, Black mutual aid wouldn't be enough. Newly freed Blacks still faced enormous economic obstacles after the Civil War— and not just because of the rise of Jim Crow in the post-

Reconstruction South. By the late nineteenth century, the Industrial Revolution was transforming the way Americans worked and lived. Black workers needed more than Black religious organizations and mutual aid societies. They needed Black unions, too.

But they would have to wait. Randolph wouldn't succeed in integrating the labor movement until 1934. And in the meantime, the labor movement was experiencing some growing pains of its own.

The labor movement of the early industrial period looked nothing like it does today. It was a period of experimentation, and one that saw plenty of failure.

Black workers found a brief ally in the Knights of Labor, one of the earliest successful efforts to unite America's countless craft unions and guilds under one umbrella. Founded in 1869 as a secret society of tailors in Philadelphia, the Knights of Labor took a wide view of who was a worker: anyone could join, as long as they weren't a lawyer, a banker, or a member of a few other excluded professions. As a consequence, the Knights of Labor got big fast, growing to as many as 700,000 members by its peak in the mid-1880s. It was one of the first major national labor organizations in America that allowed Blacks to join, and at its peak it had as many as 60,000 Black members.

But this early integration of the labor movement was short-lived. As successful as the Knights of Labor was, it was in some ways still operating with a nineteenth-century mindset in a world that was barreling headlong into the twentieth. Its internal organizational structures were weak, and it didn't have the infrastructure to leverage its commanding membership numbers. Not only that, but the union didn't have a good idea of what it would want to do with that leverage even if it had it. Without a clear goal or mission, the Knights of Labor flourished briefly before vanishing entirely. By the end of the nineteenth century, most of its membership had been lost to a new organization: the American Federation of Labor (AFL).

Founded in 1886, the AFL took a different approach to scale. Its founder, Samuel Gompers, a Jewish immigrant from London who started out as a cigar maker, believed that the only way to build leverage and power was by encouraging the most skilled, and thus the most irreplaceable, workers to strike. Gompers believed in creating strong institutions, funded by a robust economic mechanism: dues. He thought the only way to survive the booms and busts of early industrial capitalism was by employing a strategy called "business unionism." When times were good, the AFL would use the funds from members' dues to strategically disperse strike funds (payments to cover workers' basic needs while they were on strike). When times were bad, the AFL would use those dues to provide benefits.

Gompers's AFL left Black workers with nowhere to turn. The AFL was a largely white, even racist, organization. And Gompers himself became virulently anti-immigrant in his later years, especially against the Chinese. His AFL was a flawed institution, and he was a flawed man.

But I have also seen the field of labor history cite his flaws as reasons to ignore his strategic insights altogether. As with Pierre-Joseph Proudhon, the anti-Semitic French anarchist who gave us the word "mutualism," just because Gompers was limited doesn't mean we can't learn from him. "What does labor want?" Gompers famously asked. "We want more schoolhouses and less jails; more books and less arsenals; more learning and less vice; more constant work and less crime; more leisure and less greed; more justice and less revenge." The irony is that Gompers's organizational genius made the AFL into an institution that was capable of perfecting itself over time. His structural insights—that it would be impossible to stand up to employers without the buy-in and solidarity of the most skilled, most irreplaceable workers, and that a union should strike during prosperity and provide benefits during depressions—would go on to be successfully leveraged by the labor movement for decades to come. The AFL continued to grow and thrive, and soon became an increasingly important part of the fabric of progressivism in the United States.

It's here that A. Philip Randolph's story and the story of the labor movement intersect. In 1925, a group of Pullman porters—attendants on long-range railroad sleeping cars employed by the Pullman Company—voted to unionize, and they elected Randolph as their president. The Brotherhood of Sleeping Car Porters was born.

Being a Pullman porter was in some ways an enviable job for a recently freed Black worker. Some historians credit the porters with helping members of the first generation of freed Blacks enter the middle class. But the pay and working conditions were deplorable. Among other indignities, white patrons called every porter "George," after the company's president, George Pullman, no matter what the porter's real name was.

Randolph fought the Pullman Company for higher salaries and more humane hours, and he put in an application for the Brotherhood of Sleeping Car Porters to join the AFL, despite its racist past. Randolph himself was no fan of Gompers's AFL—he once called the AFL "a machine for the propagation of race prejudice"—but he also recognized the importance of getting his porters into a larger ecosystem of labor organizations. Joining it would legitimize the porters' union in the eyes of the Pullman Company, and it would help Black workers begin to build the power they would need to win bigger victories in the future.

Randolph's efforts as the head of the Brotherhood of Sleeping Car Porters were boosted by a 1926 federal law that allowed railroad workers to unionize, and that year membership in the Brotherhood rose to include a majority of black porters in America: 5,763 members. But Randolph faced setbacks, too. In 1928, his application to the AFL was rejected, and he was instead offered a compromise: the AFL agreed to recognize local unions of Sleeping Car Porters in specific cities but refused to recognize the Brotherhood as a national organization. Nevertheless, it was a start. Over the next six years, it gave Randolph an entry point to conversations and negotiations at AFL conventions that he wouldn't otherwise have been a part of.

After years of dogged organizing, the Brotherhood of Sleeping Car Porters finally won a charter to the once exclusively white American Federation of Labor in 1934, becoming the first Black union ever to do so. Randolph had succeeded in integrating a Black union into the wider labor movement, and when he won a major victory over the Pullman Company a few years later, in 1937, he was catapulted into the national spotlight as an advocate for Black workers' rights.

Bigger challenges and bigger victories were still ahead. By

1941, the specter of a second world war was on the horizon, and with it an urgent need for workers in the armed services and defense industries. Black workers had historically been shut out of these industries, and Randolph saw that responding to this need could be an opportunity to get some of the first national legislation passed to protect Black workers. Fresh off his victory over the Pullman Company, Randolph had the national visibility and clout to stand up to the Roosevelt administration.

But he couldn't do it alone, and it's here that Bayard Rustin, the man who would decades later stand next to him at the Lincoln Memorial, reenters the story.

Bayard Rustin was born in West Chester, Pennsylvania, in 1912 and raised by his grandparents. His grandmother was a Quaker and an early member of the NAACP, and his grandfather belonged to the AME Church. Rustin stayed affiliated with both churches as he grew up and years later joined a Quaker church when living in New York City.

In 1941, Randolph, working alongside Rustin, began to spread the word that a March on Washington, a massive national demonstration of Black workers, would be organized unless Roosevelt passed legislation ending segregation in the military and defense industries. Randolph issued these demands to Roosevelt himself in a meeting in the Oval Office, and Roosevelt caved. On June 25, 1941, Roosevelt issued Executive Order 8802, banning segregation in defense jobs— the first time the government had prohibited discriminatory hiring practices. Satisfied that they had won a landmark victory, Randolph called off the March.

But Rustin, who had poured himself into making preparations for the March, was not appeased. He was convinced that Roosevelt's order, which prohibited discrimination in defense industries but not in the military itself, didn't go far enough. Rustin and Randolph had a falling-out, and in the forties and early fifties Rustin threw himself into progressive work: social justice, reform, and nonviolent demonstrations. He worked on behalf of the Japanese Americans suffering in internment camps in California during World War II; he was arrested in Tennessee in 1942 for sitting in the front of a bus; and after the war, in 1947, he organized the Journey of Reconciliation, a two-week bus trip through the South to challenge segregation on the bus lines that was a precursor of the Freedom Rides of the 1960s. Through it all, he was controversially (and admirably) outspoken and even defiant about his homosexuality, and in 1953 he was arrested for a sexual encounter. Later in his life, he told a reporter that "it was an absolute necessity for me to declare homosexuality, because if I didn't, I was a part of the prejudice that was a part of the effort to destroy me."

I recently spoke to Rustin's surviving partner, Walter Naegle, who told me that Rustin believed his greatest legacy was connecting nonviolence, which he would have first encountered through his Quakerism, with the civil rights movement. In 1948, Rustin traveled to India to learn about Gandhi, the Salt March, and Gandhi's theories of nonviolence directly from Gandhi's followers. (Gandhi had died earlier that year.) Rustin brought these lessons home with him to the United States, and when the 1955 arrest of Rosa Parks led to the Montgomery bus boycott, he shared what he had learned with a new figure: Dr. Martin Luther King, Jr., whose position as the leader of the boycott was establishing him as the public face of the civil rights movement in America. "I think it's fair to say that Dr. King's view of non-violent tactics was almost non-existent when the boycott began," Rustin later said.

Rustin and Randolph's falling-out didn't last long. Years later, Rustin remembered sheepishly going to see his mentor for the first time in two years at his office in New York City: "As I was ushered in, there [Randolph] was, distinguished and dapper as ever, with arms outstretched, waiting to greet me, the way he had done a decade ago. Motioning me to sit down with that same sweep of his arm, he looked at me, and in a calm, even voice, said: 'Bayard, where have you been? You know that I have needed you.'" What Randolph would need Rustin for most was one of the most ambitious public demonstrations in history, one that would call on both men's deep experiences in the labor movement.

By early 1961, Randolph and Rustin were working together on the idea of a new March on Washington, a massive, non-violent demonstration that would focus the attention of the president and Congress on the civil rights movement, and would bring together a vast mutualist constituency drawing on both men's experiences. To succeed, the March would need representatives from a wide constellation of Black churches, which were the backbone of the movement, prominent labor leaders, and the leaders of civil rights organizations all to coordinate their efforts and unite behind a single message.

By the summer of 1963, they had put together an organizing committee made up of ten leaders from every corner of America's robust mutualist sector: the executive director of the National Catholic Conference for Interracial Justice (Mathew Ahmann); the vice chairman of the Commission on Race Relations of the National Council of Churches of Christ in America (Eugene Carson Blake); the president of the Southern Christian Leadership Conference (Martin Luther King, Jr.); the chairman of the American Jewish Congress (Joachim Prinz); the national director of the Congress of Racial Equality (James Farmer); the chairman of the Student Nonviolent Coordinating Committee (John Lewis); the executive secretary of the National Association for the Advancement of Colored People (Roy Wilkins); the executive director of the National Urban League (Whitney Young); the president of the United Auto Workers and chairman of the AFL-CIO's Industrial Union Department (Walter Reuther); and the president of the Negro American Labor Council (Randolph himself).

Even if Rustin and Randolph hadn't used the word "mutualist" to describe the massive grassroots ecosystem they were drawing on, it's clear they understood that a diversity of mature mutualist organizations would be essential to the March's success. In an organizing manual distributed before the March, Rustin specifically invited the support and sponsorship of mutualist organizations and declined the sponsorship of anyone else:

> *Organizational* sponsorship is invited only from the established Civil Rights organizations, from major religious and fraternal groups, and from labor unions. Such groups are invited to form committees, to sponsor the March, and to send delegations to Washington in their own names.

Rustin understood that these organizations were sophisticated, mature institutions with robust internal organizational structures and a culture of reciprocity born of decades of solidarity. They had activist members who were committed, and leaders with minds for logistics who could organize their own constituents and fund their own trips to the Capitol. These were institutions that understood how to move the levers of power and engage in the political process, institutions that could tolerate a variety of different views and that recognized there was strength in solidarity nonetheless.

The day's success was largely due to Randolph's and Rustin's organizational genius and eye for detail. "We planned out precisely the number of toilets that would be needed for a quarter of a million people," Rustin later remembered, "how many doctors, how many first aid stations, what people should bring with them to eat in their lunches." He circulated the twelve-page "Organizing Manual No. 2"—offering instructions for those coming to Washington via plane, train, bus, or automobile—and both men knew they could rely on the mutualist organizations to carry these instructions out to the letter. Their suggestions for what food to bring read as follows:

> We urge all marchers to take 2 box lunches—one for midday, one for supper. These box lunches should be kept simple and balanced. Exclude perishable or spoilable foods—no mayonnaise or salads, for example. We suggest:
>> peanut butter and jelly sandwiches
>> an apple or other fruit
>> a brownie or plain cake
>> a soft drink.

. . .

By the late morning of August 28, 1963, it was clear the March was going to be a phenomenal success. The final estimates of the crowd size were somewhere between 250,000 and 300,000, making it the largest political demonstration in American history up to that point. And to the relief of Rustin, the March went off peacefully, securing its place alongside Gandhi's Salt March as one of the most important nonviolent demonstrations in history.

Randolph delivered the day's opening remarks, and after King's speech Rustin took the podium to read the March's list of demands. That list, numbering ten demands in all, included that Congress pass "comprehensive and effective *civil rights legislation*," that schools be desegregated within the year, and that an executive order be issued banning racial discrimination in any federally supported housing. The last four demands were economic and called for sweeping reform that would affect workers of all races:

7. A massive federal program to train and place all unemployed workers—Negro and white—on meaningful and dignified jobs at decent wages.
8. A national *minimum wage* act that will give all Americans a decent standard of living. (Government surveys show that anything less than $2.00 an hour fails to do this.)
9. A broadened *Fair Labor Standards Act* to include all areas of employment which are presently excluded.
10. A federal *Fair Employment Practices Act* barring discrimination by federal, state and municipal governments,

and by employers, contractors, employment agencies, and trade unions.

For Randolph, who was in his seventies at the time, the March on Washington was the culmination of a lifetime of trying to bring Black workers into the broader labor movement. For Rustin, it brought together his work for economic equality and his Quaker instinct for nonviolent change.

Randolph and Rustin certainly didn't begin their careers imagining that one day they would be speaking to a quarter of a million people on the National Mall. Like most effective leaders, they started out by solving problems. That decades later they found themselves at the helm of one of the most important social movements in American history is a testament to the power of what even the smallest, most local institutions can eventually achieve when they come together with a common purpose. They can change the world in a way that isolated individuals could never do.

In my own decades of organizing freelancers, I've realized that mutualist organizations are often the source of big ideas, but the mutualist ecosystems they grow into are where profound social change begins. This change has always been deliberate and planned—and in every era it has been fueled by the local community institutions that give major social movements their infrastructure, their financing, and the logistical base that makes it possible to organize.

Tomorrow's change will emerge from the ground up when today's visionaries build lasting structures around their ideas—and when they look for ways to connect to other social movements, just like A. Philip Randolph and Bayard

Rustin did. We'll recognize these new leaders when we see them: they'll have a vision, but they'll also have a strategy. Their vision will have grown out of the problems they solved for their own communities, but their work won't be done until the institutions they create are strong enough to outlast those founding leaders. To create the mutualist future on which tomorrow's social contract will rest, we need to start by building. Because builders are the ones who change the world.

PART II

THE MUTUALIST FUTURE

CHAPTER 6

What Does Labor Want?

or, We Are All Workers

W hat does it mean to be a worker? The answer is simple: a worker is someone who works. Unless you can afford not to (and most of us can't), the only way to put food on your table, clothes on your body, and a roof over your head is to exchange your time, labor, or expertise for a wage.

Work can be unskilled or skilled, knowledge work or physical labor, paid fairly or poorly. It can happen behind a computer screen or the wheel of a tractor. It can occur as part of a formal employment relationship or not. None of these distinctions change the fact that working is something that Americans of all classes, colors, and creeds do every day. The vast majority of us need to work in order to live.

But changes in technology and the economy are altering the way we work, so that an increasing number of American workers are left out of the structures the labor movement created almost one hundred years ago to help them. Freelancers are on the front lines of this change. Working more than one job, trying to juggle the costs of living such as healthcare, student debt, homeownership, and raising children, freelancers are consumed with anxiety and exhaustion. And even successful freelancers are shouldering unbearable amounts of risk: 59 percent of independent contractors live paycheck to paycheck, and 75 percent worry they don't save enough for emergencies or retirement. In the first half of this book, we explored mutualism: what it is, where it can be found in our past, and what it has accomplished at scale. Now we'll see how to bring about the mutualist future—a future we'll need in order to replace our vanishing safety net. But first, let's dig a little more deeply into one problem we're facing. With no institutions to support us, today's workers face every day alone.

Loneliness isn't just an inconvenience. It's an existential threat to the American workforce. Feeling alone can be deadly. The following story, about a taxi driver named Douglas Schifter, an independent contractor who was left out of the changing economy, comes from a haunting 2018 *New York* magazine feature by Jessica Bruder, who learned much of this by talking to Schifter's brother George—as well as from Schifter's own suicide note, posted publicly to Facebook the morning he died.

Growing up in Canarsie, Brooklyn, in the 1960s, Douglas Schifter probably hadn't planned to spend his life behind the wheel of a taxi. He was introverted and bookish, but when he flunked out of high school after failing gym, he needed a job. He started out driving one of New York City's iconic yellow cabs, but by the 1990s he decided he was due for a promotion. He sold the medallion, upgraded his wardrobe, and went to work driving Lincoln Town Cars for a black-car service called XYZ. "I was the most skilled and experienced driver to my knowledge in the business," he later boasted on Facebook. "I had almost 5 million miles experience, driven through five hurricanes and over 50 deep snow and blizzard conditions. I have driven over 100 world famous celebrities. . . . I was a top chauffeur with the greatest limo company of all time."

Eventually, in 2004, thanks to his six-figure income from driving black cars, Schifter was able to afford a home of his own next to a state forest in the Pocono Mountains, where he made his own ice cream and smoked meat. But life wasn't easy. When Schifter shattered his hip after slipping on some ice, he was unable to work for three months. With no unemployment insurance (and likely without disability), this meant three months without pay—a setback that, in spite of his good income, Schifter couldn't afford. He returned to work too early, and a week later a fender bender in Times Square caused even more damage to his still-tender hip. He was forced to take another six weeks off and had to declare bankruptcy.

"Unable to spare the time to drive home to the Poconos," Jessica Bruder wrote, "Schifter slept in his car most nights, parking at a rest stop near the next morning's job. He kept two suits in rotation, making frequent visits to a dry cleaner. He showered at truck stops." Hanging on by a thread both physically and financially, Schifter began putting in longer hours and resting even less. Though he wasn't great with money, he was a hard worker, and smart. He might even have pulled himself out of the tailspin if a new technology hadn't set its sights squarely on workers just like him.

It was around this time that the founder of a San Francisco startup called StumbleUpon needed a ride on New

Year's Eve. He hired a local black-car service much like Schifter's and a few days later got a bill for $800. It got this tech executive thinking: What if you could share the cost of hiring a private driver for a night with a few other people, but pay only for the rides you took? He found a partner and a business was born: an on-demand livery cab service dispatched directly through your brand-new smartphone. The rest, of course, is Silicon Valley history. The more the co-founders of Uber looked into the state of the taxicab and livery car market, the more they saw a hoary, slow-moving industry that could be easily outflanked.

The taxi industry was particularly attractive to Uber because taxi drivers had come to be classified as independent contractors. This means that they were responsible for paying their own taxes, buying their own health and disability insurance, performing their own vehicle maintenance, and setting up their own retirement accounts. Plus, as independent contractors, they had no formal mechanism to unionize. It would cost Uber nothing to hire these drivers and take a cut of their earnings. Uber cars soon flooded New York City, and before anyone in the city government realized what was happening, the economy that governed the New York taxi industry had changed.

"Everywhere he looked, Schifter saw the signs of an impending taxi apocalypse," Bruder wrote in her *New York* magazine profile. "One cabdriver told Schifter that he used to work five days a week and take home $1,000. Now he was driving seven days a week and taking home $800. . . . In 2015, Schifter spent an entire Wednesday evening on call, and for the first time in his four decades of driving, not a single job came through." In the fall of 2017, the engine in his GMC Yukon XL Denali gave out. Behind on his mortgage payments and $75,000 in debt, with an expensive car repair hanging over his head, Schifter faced the indignity of losing his Poconos home. He became depressed and began talking with his brother George about wanting to die.

At 4:33 A.M. on February 5, 2018, Schifter posted a long public letter to Facebook. The day before, he'd gotten into a rented black Nissan sedan, left his house, and driven east. His destination: City Hall in lower Manhattan. Schifter's Facebook letter is worth finding and reading in its entirety (it's easy to search for online); he could see the change in America's social contract lucidly. "Forget about a great country," he wrote, "we are not even good people if we do not care for others in need. . . . I don't know how else to try to make a difference other than a public display of a most private affair."

At 7:10 A.M. on Monday, February 5, a blast rang out in downtown Manhattan. Without even taking his seatbelt off, Schifter had shot himself in the face with a shotgun. Jessica Bruder described what happened next: "Police responded, taping off the scene. Traffic was halted on the Manhattan-bound side of the Brooklyn Bridge. The bomb squad came to check for explosives. All they found in the car was Schifter, lifeless in a crisp white shirt and dress pants. Next to him, inside a Ziploc bag, was a photograph of a clean-shaven kid standing in front of the American flag. It was a photo of George, from his days in basic training in the Air Force; on his recent visit, he had urged Doug to keep it with him, so he wouldn't feel alone."

Loneliness: it's a word I hear all the time. Douglas Schifter's death is part of a larger trend that isn't unique to him or even to his industry. It is the result of a half century that has seen the systematic dismantling of the safety net and the atomization of the workforce to such an extent that today's workers have nowhere to turn in periods of uncertainty. Over the past three decades, employers like Uber have increasingly relied on a stable of independent contractors to do the work that was once done by full-time employees. This is also true for industries across the socioeconomic spectrum, for workers from taxi drivers to software engineers, copywriters to consultants, workers we used to think of as solidly middle- or even upper-middle-class.

How did we get here? Beginning with the New Deal, America's safety net was built around "employees," a legal category of workers that is distinct from "independent contractors." Under the most important piece of labor legislation ever passed in the United States, the National Labor Relations Act of 1935 (the Wagner Act), only "employees" are covered by labor protections. Under the Civil Rights Act of 1964, only "employees" are protected from discrimination. And under state unemployment laws, only "employees" are eligible to collect unemployment insurance. Tomorrow's safety net can't just cover "employees." It needs to be extended to cover workers of all kinds.

Freelancers—the most rapidly growing segment of today's workforce—are the most exposed. And yet many middle-class freelancers I know don't believe the labor movement is for them at all. They think it's for people who are needier than they are, even though these same freelancers struggle with a remarkably similar litany of complaints in their own economic lives: irregular income, expensive healthcare premiums, little to no rainy day fund, lack of available cash on hand for a down payment on an apartment or a house, and anxiety about giving the best to their children. The complaints and aspirations of many of today's precarious workers are exactly the same, from the least to the most skilled, from the lowest- to the highest-wage earners, but most of us believe that we have nothing in common.

This misconception, that unionization is only for low-wage workers, couldn't be further from the truth. Unions were historically intended to protect *all* workers. Low-wage and middle-wage workers need to stand together. Without this solidarity, vulnerable workers will not have the leverage they need to achieve meaningful change for themselves.

Why do so many middle-class workers believe the labor movement isn't for them? The division of workers into "employees" and "independent contractors" is just one example of a larger trend that dates back to the Taft-Hartley Act of 1947: an attempt by anti-labor capitalism to weaken the labor movement from within by dividing the workforce. Over the past half century, politicians, policy makers, labor leaders, foundations, and workers alike have internalized these divisions. Today, rather than asking if someone is a worker who deserves our society's protection, we ask instead what kind of worker they are first: Blue- or white-collar? Low- or high-wage? Skilled or unskilled? Knowledge or service worker? Employee or independent contractor?

But in 2021, if you're a worker of any type, you're exposed. Even for employees, the world has changed since the 1950s, when the workforce was one-third unionized, your pension plan paid you a guaranteed amount upon retirement, and the workday was limited to eight hours and the workweek to five days. Today, only 10.3 percent of workers are unionized, retirement is wholly dependent on the ups and downs of the stock market, and the workweek includes nights and weekends.

Work is changing whether you're an employee or an independent contractor. So the safety net needs to change with it. Workers need to be protected by a safety net that isn't tied to their workplace and that is as mobile as they are. Mutualist organizations are the natural place to begin to build these mobile benefits, and the labor movement will be the cornerstone of that mutualist safety net. After all, the labor movement has built the safety net not once, but twice: first in the Progressive Era by unions like the ILGWU in the 1910s and '20s, and then again after the New Deal through the middle of the century.

But to build the new safety net, we need a strong labor movement. And for the labor movement to be strong, it will have to serve all workers. In 2021, that means all of us: from low-wage to high-wage workers, from Uber drivers with precarious incomes to middle-class freelance graphic designers, from independent contractors to employees. We have to realize that we're stronger when we stand together, especially in the face of forces that are conspiring to make us feel more alone than ever before. Only then can we begin to build the institutions we need.

The story of how the working class became divided in the first place starts in the years leading up to the last major crisis of work: the Great Depression.

Histories of the New Deal, such as Steven Greenhouse's excellent book *Beaten Down, Worked Up,* often begin with an early-spring weekend in Washington Square Park in Manhattan. It was Saturday, March 25, 1911. A woman named Frances Perkins, who had recently moved to New York from Philadelphia, was enjoying an afternoon with a friend in a townhouse just off Washington Square when they heard screams and the roar of fire engines. They rushed out into the street, and what they saw was horrifying: a fire had broken out in a sweatshop near the top of a loft building on the east side of the park, home to the Triangle Shirtwaist Company. The workers, mostly young girls, had been locked in by their supervisors. Many couldn't reach the stairs or the roof, and the only way out of the inferno was through the ninth-story windows. It was a grisly scene. Perkins, along with hundreds of passersby, watched the helpless workers line up on the window ledges, waiting for their turn to hurl themselves to their death. One man kissed a woman next to him before they fell one after the other. "They would hit the sidewalk," Perkins remembered decades later, in a 1964 lecture at Cornell University. ". . . Every one of them was killed. Everybody who jumped was killed."

One hundred and forty-six people died. With that day seared into her memory, Perkins dedicated herself to pro-worker legislation in New York, to make sure nothing like the Triangle Shirtwaist fire ever happened again. She worked alongside a young state senator named Robert Wagner as the primary investigator on the new Factory Investigating Commission, and together they were tireless. Their work led to sweeping laws in New York City aimed at preventing similar disasters, and Perkins later said that she found particular satisfaction in knowing that "in New York I could see a fire escape and say: I did that." Years later, she would remember the Triangle Shirtwaist fire as "the day the New Deal was born."

But Perkins wasn't the only one galvanized by the harsh realities of industrial capitalism in the years before the New Deal. Progressive innovation was happening all around her. Labor leaders and worker organizations were undergoing a Cambrian explosion of mutualist experimentation, solving problems and seeing what worked. There was no one right way to organize workers, so labor leaders were throwing solutions against the wall and seeing which ones stuck.

These were the years when my grandfather's ILGWU and Sidney Hillman's Amalgamated Clothing Workers of America, the two great "needle unions," were building the mutualist ecosystems discussed in chapter 4: union banks, houses, healthcare clinics, schools, vacation destinations. They were beta testing a new organizing strategy inspired by Samuel Gompers's strategic insight that the most skilled workers were the ones who had the most leverage with employers. But they took that strategy one step further: What if they didn't stop with organizing just the skilled workers? What if, instead, they *used* those skilled workers as a wedge to establish gains for everyone else? Instead of organizing workers around a given craft, what if they organized them around an entire industry? What if furriers, seamstresses, tailors, makers of skirts, bras, buttons, or skirt hoops—workers from the lowest-wage earners to the most skilled—were all part of the same organization?

These new vertically integrated labor organizations were called industrial unions, and by the 1930s there were industrial unions for steelworkers, autoworkers, rubber workers, and even screenwriters and actors. It was an industrial-sized mutualist strategy designed to take on the industrial-sized exploitation rampant in the now industrial-sized economy, and it worked. These early industrial unions marked the begin-

ning of the modern labor movement and were the precur-
sors of the labor unions many of us grew up with.

In *Beaten Down, Worked Up,* Steven Greenhouse tracks
Frances Perkins's rise through the ranks of New York State's
progressive politics. By the time of the Great Depression in
1929, she was working for Franklin Roosevelt, then governor
of New York. With fifteen million Americans unemployed
and no end to the suffering in sight, the country was losing
patience with the ham-handed response of President Herbert Hoover. Roosevelt, by contrast, was talking about unemployment insurance and pensions for the elderly, and in
Albany the legislature passed a massive emergency economic
relief package to help New Yorkers weather the downturn.
"New York became a national leader in creating not just a
relief program but a public works program to put the jobless
back to work," Greenhouse writes. "In 1932, the Democratic
Party nominated Roosevelt as its presidential candidate,
largely because as New York's governor he had led the way
with innovative programs to help the poor and jobless."

Roosevelt won the election by an overwhelming margin
that fall, which meant a new opportunity was coming for
Perkins as well. Roosevelt wanted her to be secretary of
labor, but she was hesitant to accept the position. After all,
she'd never led a union, and many believed that the secretary
of labor should be a former union leader. As Greenhouse
notes, Roosevelt wouldn't have any of it, telling her that "it
was time to consider all working people, organized and unorganized."

Perkins had a sweeping vision of a Nordic-style nationalized safety net, complete with health insurance and medical
care, and this massive effort—change at a scale that only an
institution as large as the federal government could bring

about—formed the first part of Roosevelt's response to the Depression. "I see no reason why every child, from the day he is born, shouldn't be a member of the social security system. From the cradle to the grave they ought to be in a social insurance system," Roosevelt famously said. Although Social Security was the only one of the social insurance reforms that Perkins and Roosevelt managed to pass in its entirety, the success of Roosevelt's top-down approach to social change via government programs created the sweeping national initiatives—Civilian Conservation Corps, Works Progress Administration, and so on—that we associate with the New Deal today.

For most Americans, this is where the story of the New Deal begins and ends. But I see another important element to the story. Roosevelt recognized the limits of what government could accomplish on its own. He realized he needed organizations on the ground, too. Rather than build new institutions from scratch, he looked at the ecosystem of mutualist organizations that already existed and realized that unions were the perfect tools to find workers where they already were.

The New Deal was about increasing workers' standard of living, but to address this issue FDR didn't issue a law ordering employers to pay higher wages. Instead, he empowered unions to fight for higher wages. He didn't regulate which part of the country or which industries should unionize. Instead, he built a system by which workers in almost any industry could petition the government to have a union election at their workplace. He constructed a system in which workers could build the institutions they needed themselves. And build them they did. Union membership increased from 7.5 percent of the workforce in 1930 to 35 percent by 1955, and unions—each an individual node of mutualist organization that touched thousands if not tens of thousands of workers— stabilized the workforce and began to pull America out of the Depression.

On July 5, 1935, Roosevelt signed the National Labor Relations Act into law. It bore the fingerprints of Perkins and her colleague from her days investigating New York City factories, now U.S. senator Robert Wagner, who gave the law its other nickname, the Wagner Act. It was the first of a series of laws passed over the following years that would enshrine, protect, define, and bolster the labor movement, and in particular the strategy of industrial unionism. Whereas before the law, organized labor had been a diverse and idiosyncratic mutualist movement that was constantly experimenting, after the Wagner Act unions became something more standardized. They had a specific purpose, specific goals, specific procedures and rules for how to achieve those goals, and specific requirements for membership. On signing the Wagner Act, Roosevelt said:

A better relationship between labor and management is the high purpose of this Act. By assuring the employees the right of collective bargaining it fosters the development of the employment contract on a sound and equitable basis. By providing an orderly procedure for determining who is entitled to represent the employees, it aims to remove one of the chief causes of wasteful economic strife. By preventing practices which tend to destroy the independence of labor, it seeks, for every worker within its scope, that freedom of choice and action which is justly his.

By protecting the right to collective bargaining, by exempting unions from antitrust laws that prevent most groups from taking collective action and setting standard wage rates, and by ensuring that union employees would not be subject to anti-union activity, Roosevelt had in effect given unions a "job" in the post–New Deal economy. By putting a legal structure around their right to collectively bargain, Roosevelt had given unions a mandate—to bargain for higher wages—while also giving their economic model a regulatory backstop. In exchange for offering the valuable service of collective bargaining, unions were able to charge dues that were significant enough to allow them to sustain their organizations. The New Deal created the business model that let unions thrive through the middle of the twentieth century.

But notice that Roosevelt said "for every worker within its scope." That's because the Wagner Act also defined who was eligible for the law's protections. In a short section headed "Definitions," the act explicitly excluded domestic workers and agricultural workers—workers who were usually people of color—from having the right to unionize. So who *was* eligible to unionize? The language was deliberately vague: "any employee." The interpretation of what exactly made a worker an employee was left to future generations to litigate. And litigate they would: this short paragraph is where labor legislation first began to divide the workforce. As the list of exclusions was modified, added to, and tweaked, it eventually became a tool used to hollow out the Wagner Act from within.

But at the peak of the Great Depression, tying the National Labor Relations Act to "any employee" made sense: it was through the unit of the employee that Roosevelt could reach the largest number of Americans. And for many decades, the aggregate effect of the National Labor Relations Act was to give firm legal support to the strategy of industrial unionism, a strategy that lifted wages and working conditions for a record number of Americans. Backed by the legal protections of the Wagner Act, the strategy worked: over the following decades, labor leaders strategically identified and then leveraged their most skilled workers as a bargaining chip to unite whole industries, from low-wage earners to skilled workers, succeeding where past attempts at unionization had failed—in no small part because, at the time, most of the American workforce was eligible to be unionized.

The success of this period of the labor movement is perhaps best exemplified by the early autoworkers' strikes. Workers in the auto industry had been trying to unionize for decades, but the old craft unions, made up of workers who had specific skills such as machining or upholstering, had no leverage in the industrial era. Most autoworkers had become as interchangeable as the parts of the new assembly-line cars they built, and strike after strike had failed. By the middle of the 1930s, conditions in one General Motors plant in Flint, Michigan, were so bad that workers began to drop unconscious from the heat on the shop floor, forcing their colleagues to step over them to continue working.

But by late 1936, with the legal protection of the Wagner Act in place, a new union called the United Automobile Workers (UAW) was putting into motion a series of strikes that strategically united GM's workforce. A local Flint plant, Fisher No. 1, contained one of GM's only molds, or dies, which stamped huge sheets of metal into shape to produce the body of a car. Shut down the die, and you'd cripple the entire supply chain. On December 30, 1936, Flint workers did just that by turning Fisher No. 1 into occupied territory.

They refused to leave, and they set up an ersatz system of governance to keep their temporary encampment running: shifts for lookouts and guards, a system to facilitate the delivery of food and other supplies, even a temporary postal service. The Great Sit-Down Strike, as it was later called, crippled GM's production schedule and forced the company to recognize the UAW's legitimacy.

Two years later, Walter Reuther, who had just assumed leadership of the UAW's General Motors department and who decades later would share the stage with Bayard Rustin and A. Philip Randolph at the March on Washington in 1963, put that legitimacy to the test. This time, it was the tool and die workers, skilled machinists who made and operated the giant dies, who struck. It was 1939, and GM was trying to roll out its 1940 models by the end of the summer. Though the tool and die workers made up only a small percentage of GM's total workforce, without these skilled workers production ground to a halt. GM was forced to negotiate, paving the way for major changes for all of GM's workers.

These strikes were a victory not only for the UAW but also for the whole strategy of industrial unionism. As labor historian Nelson Lichtenstein put it in his biography of Walter Reuther, these strikes "represented one of the industrial union movement's most significant steps toward the New Deal era's transformation of the American class structure. . . . By 1960 relative wage differentials within GM's production workforce had declined by 60 percent, a pattern replicated throughout unionized industry." The industrial union strategy, that everyone in a given industry should stand together regardless of skill or wage—in other words, that all workers deserved to be unionized—was paying off. But this kind of worker solidarity didn't just exist within industries. It also existed *between* industries and included alliances that might surprise us today.

In the late 1950s, the Black and Puerto Rican women who worked as nurse's aides in New York City's hospitals "earned so little . . . that many needed supplementary relief from the Welfare Department to feed, clothe and house their families," *The New York Times* observed years later. "They had neither Blue Cross nor sick pay insurance, and it was a tragic joke in the hospitals that none of their nonprofessional employees could afford to be sick." Many of these women belonged to Local 1199 of the Drug, Hospital and Health Care Employees Union, the same union I worked for after college, when, while employed as a dietary aide, I helped organize a nursing home.

A man named Leon Davis, a Jewish immigrant and communist sympathizer, had formed Local 1199 in 1932 to represent these low-skilled, low-wage, replaceable workers. Davis was a fierce believer in social justice for people of color, and by the 1950s he also had an ally in an unexpected place. In 1959, Davis led a major strike against all of New York City's major hospitals: Mount Sinai, Beth Israel, Bronx, Lenox Hill, Brooklyn Jewish, Beth David, and Flower–Fifth Avenue. On the picket lines outside the hospitals, the Black and Puerto Rican women of Local 1199 were joined by a squad of white men, all working-class electricians from the International Brotherhood of Electrical Workers, Local 3. They were led by a tough-talking former electrician named Harry Van Arsdale, Jr.

Local 1199's strike, which lasted forty-six days, succeeded in no small part because Local 3's electricians stood in solidarity with the hospital workers, who had less bargaining power. It was an alliance of both pragmatism and principle:

union density in New York City was good for Local 3 and Local 1199 alike. But it was also simply the right thing to do. Harry Van Arsdale and Leon Davis went on to enjoy a friendship that would last for decades, forged from a shared devotion to improving the lives of their unions' members. In 1970, Davis remembered their years of striking together, saying, "Van Arsdale couldn't have worked harder to rally help if it were his own electricians on strike."

Protected by the Wagner Act, industrial union strategies like Walter Reuther's tool and die workers' strike and Davis and Van Arsdale's union solidarity ensured that through the middle of the twentieth century, a whole generation of workers not only enjoyed unprecedented prosperity and security, but also shared something perhaps more essential: camaraderie and solidarity with their fellow workers.

So what happened between the 1950s—when white working-class electricians and low-wage Black and Puerto Rican immigrants stood together on the streets of New York because they recognized that they were stronger together—and today?

The decline in solidarity begins where the Wagner Act ends: with its list of excluded workers and its vague definition of the word "employee."

You can't read a history of the labor movement without encountering an analysis of just how devastating the Taft-Hartley Act, passed by Congress only twelve years after the Wagner Act, proved to be. Taft-Hartley crippled labor by restricting the rights of unions—banning certain kinds of strikes, putting limits on the ways unions could organize, and laying the groundwork for today's so-called "right to work" laws. But it was with that list of exclusions that the Taft-

Hartley Act really gutted the identity of the American work-force.

First, Taft-Hartley introduced the word "supervisors" in this list. Supervisors—better-paid, harder-to-replace, often white-collar professionals, whose skills were social and managerial, and who enjoyed stronger bargaining power with employers—were now forbidden to stand with their low-skilled, low-wage fellow workers. As labor historian Nelson Lichtenstein notes in his history of the labor movement, *State of the Union*, excluding supervisors from the protections of the Wagner Act was a crushing defeat:

> The unionization of finance, engineering, insurance, banking, and other private-sector service industries proved virtually impossible with the ban on supervisory unionism. The ranks of these white-collar and service-sector workers would swell over the next few decades . . . and by the 1990s the Census Bureau defined more workers as managerial, professional, and technical than blue-collar. Few were actually true executives or independent professionals, but the evolving labor law for the most part failed to take the new sociology of work into account. Or rather, it gave a perverse, Orwellian reading to the nation's occupational transformation, so that huge numbers of middle-wage, nonsupervisory workers, including game wardens, registered nurses, fast-food restaurant "managers," purchasing agents, dentists, medical interns, paralegals, engineers, newspaper editors, and college professors at private schools have been denied protection either by the NLRB or by the wage-and-hour provisions of the Fair Labor Standards Act.

The legislators behind Taft-Hartley shrewdly saw that one crucial way to weaken the labor movement was to remove from labor's tool kit the kind of low- and high-wage solidarity that made strikes like that of the tool and die workers so effective. With each new organizing drive, the norm that supervisory workers were not part of the rest of the working class became established—and, as a result, these workers switched from having solidarity with their fellow workers to becoming an arm of management.

Taft-Hartley also introduced the phrase "independent contractors" into the Wagner Act's list of excluded workers. But just as the Wagner Act declined to define "all employees," so, too, did Taft-Hartley fail to elaborate on what exactly made someone an "independent contractor."

So what is an independent contractor, exactly? I've been organizing freelancers for more than twenty-five years and probably know as much about independent contractors as anyone. And yet even I am still shocked by how slippery the term is. Not only is the IRS itself unclear ("There is no 'magic' or set number of factors that 'makes' the worker an employee or an independent contractor, and no one factor stands alone in making this determination," says the IRS website, unhelpfully), but the laws also vary from state to state. Defining an independent contractor should be straightforward, but it isn't.

Typically, a person is an independent contractor if they have a large amount of control over where, when, how, and with what tools they do their work. They contract (whether formally or informally) with a variety of clients, set their own hours, and work only as much as they're needed. They buy their own health insurance and pay their own income tax directly to the government. Their income can be sporadic, and they are not covered by race and gender discrimination laws. And it wasn't until COVID-19 that they became eligible for unemployment benefits. For the first time in 2020, freelancers could apply for federal money through their states, which had formerly reserved unemployment insurance benefits for employees only.

Over the past several decades, more and more workers have been classified as independent contractors. You could argue that this is for simple economic reasons, and there is some truth to this. Before today's technology made it easy to see trends in business, factory owners couldn't predict the volume of orders they'd receive in a given month, and as a consequence could predict neither how much product to keep on hand nor how much labor they needed. So they stockpiled both: labor was a fixed cost, warehouses were full, and employees were full-time. More recently, as technology has enabled companies to become more agile in predicting business needs, labor has become a variable cost. Many of the needs companies have today are short-term or project-based, and corporations simply don't require an army of full-time employees anymore.

But employers have always looked for ways to cut costs, and ever since the Wagner Act gave unions the ability to negotiate for higher wages and better working conditions, employers have been looking for ways to avoid the cost and hassle of providing them. As expensive employer-sponsored benefits like health insurance and paid time off became codified into American law and practice in the 1940s, employers began to look for ways to avoid offering these benefits. As a consequence, more and more companies began hiring freelancers and consultants to do the work that full-time employees used to do. After all, the more a company's business could be handled by temporary independent contractors, the more money its owners and shareholders could keep for themselves. Since independent contractors had been specifically excluded from the Wagner Act by Taft-Hartley, it would become almost impossible for them to stand up for themselves.

Without a clear definition of what constitutes an "employee" or an "independent contractor," the field has been wide open for employers to interpret these definitions however they like. As corporations and businesses have found increasingly creative ways to keep their workers firmly excluded from the Wagner Act, more and more of the American workforce has become ineligible to unionize.

Today, we instinctively sort ourselves by all kinds of categories—white-collar versus blue-collar, professional versus working class, deserving versus undeserving, working-class rank and file versus middle-class—while believing that all these groups don't share a similar set of interests. As a result, our ability to imagine that those with whom we disagree can still be our economic allies has eroded. The consequence of a divided workforce is not only a weakened sense of identity but also a weakened negotiating position for workers. Harry Van Arsdale's electricians and Leon Davis's hospital workers came from completely different walks of life, but they walked a picket line together because they knew that their goals— higher wages and fairer working conditions—were the same. They were all workers.

So what does it mean to be a worker today? On April 16, 2020, about a month after the COVID-19 crisis began, the S&P 500 had already bounced back 25 percent from its lows at the start of the quarantine, the NASDAQ had bounced back 24 percent, Uber stock was up 82 percent, and Amazon crested at $2,400 a share, its highest price ever. The very same day, Americans got the news that 22 million workers had filed for unemployment, dwarfing the scale of unemployment during any period since the Great Depression.

The bull run of the stock market in the years between the Great Recession of 2007–2008 and the COVID-19 pandemic obscured a truth that is obvious today but that many Americans felt in their bones as a lived experience over the past decade: although the economy was booming in the 2010s, the vast majority of us weren't prospering. You've probably seen graphs like this one, showing the stark divergence of the stock market and the actual wages of workers.

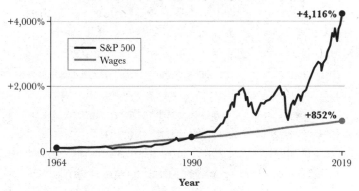

Percent Growth in S&P 500 and Production/Non-Supervisory Wages since 1964

Source: St. Louis Federal Reserve, Robert Schiller

Does a taxi driver like Douglas Schifter really have anything in common with, say, a freelance UX designer who manages to make rent on her $4,000 one-bedroom apartment in the Mission District of San Francisco? The progressive response of nonprofits, foundations, charities, Democratic elected officials, public intellectuals, and think tanks—the people in America who ostensibly support America's workers—would be "no." The "real" workers, the thinking goes, the workers worth protecting, are the low-wage and vulnerable workers, and these workers do better when their needs are addressed by nonprofits, foundations, or charities—rather than within an institutional structure that is built by the workers themselves. The upshot is that the most vulnerable workers have been deprived of their best allies, the other half of the working class, and of the institutions they need to give them real ownership of their lives.

Employers, eager to capitalize on a divided workforce, do not hesitate to prey on this misconception. When workers at Kickstarter tried to unionize in early 2019, they received the following email from their employer: "Forming a union is a great tool—for marginalized workers. Unions are historically intended to protect vulnerable members of society, and we feel the demographics of this union undermine this important function. We're concerned with the misappropriation of unions for use by privileged workers, some of whom receive compensation more than twice the average income in NYC." This "concern" couldn't be further from the truth. Kickstarter was likely concerned only that unionization by these "privileged" workers would result in a united workforce.

This view is exactly opposite that of Karl Marx, who believed that workers are defined first and foremost by their relationship to the means of production. As Marx might have said, despite their wildly differing incomes, a taxi driver and a wealthy UX designer have this in common: neither of them controls the means of production, and both of them create more value for their employers than they themselves make in income. The corporations they work for are pocketing the difference. The same can be said of the vast majority of American workers—even the most successful freelance consultants making six-figure incomes. Most of us live on this graph's bottom line, not its top line. In other words, we are all workers.

Unions were the architects of the original safety net, and they will be the cornerstone of tomorrow's as well. But without a united workforce, the labor movement will remain in retrenchment. To rebuild it, we have to reclaim the essential solidarity of all workers and recognize that the only way to renew America's social contract is to build a safety net that works for all of us, regardless of how we're classified. We must remember a principle that the labor movement was based on, but that in 2021 feels as radical as it is simple: We are all workers. And we are not alone.

CHAPTER 7

The Future of Labor

Organizing the Unorganized

Freelancers have taught me to imagine the future they'd like to see. That future, one built around their needs, has been a North Star to guide me throughout my career. In these last four chapters, I invite you to imagine the future—our mutualist future—with me.

Imagine a future in which you can take your low-cost health insurance from job to job because you get it through your organization of freelance writers rather than your employer. Imagine that you and your colleagues have a say in how this insurance works: what you want to see covered and what isn't a priority. Imagine a future in which you're embedded in a dynamic group of like-minded workers from across the globe who are asking the same questions as you every day: How do I get started? How do I find more work? Am I the only one who isn't being treated fairly or paid enough? How do I keep growing in the middle of my career? Imagine a future in which you can live wherever you choose, take on only the jobs you like, and have access to someone whose chief priority is to listen to what you need to stay relevant in your field and help you get the necessary training. Imagine trusting that this organization has your back through lows as well as highs, that it works with you to see you through major life changes like starting a family or planning for retirement. Imagine facing work every day in a way that makes you feel connected and empowered rather than alone and exposed.

None of this is far-fetched. There are new unions—and new organizations that might not even call themselves unions but nonetheless behave like the best of them—that are already pointing the way to the mutualist future. They're doing so by following four basic principles.

> First, they're not waiting for permission from the government or anyone else to start organizing. Instead, they're experimenting with ways to solve problems for their members, seeing what works, and iterating.

> Second, they're using new technologies to meet workers where they are. I call this the growing movement of *network unionism*.

> Third, they're listening to the real needs of workers, who deserve to be organized regardless of their classification.

> Fourth, they're finding ways to build power by funding themselves—though as we'll see in the next chapter, government needs to pivot to enable them to scale.

Today's workforce needs a safety net that doesn't depend on whether workers are employees or independent contractors. To become the anchor of that safety net, tomorrow's labor movement will need to meet these workers where they already are—on their phones where they're using platforms to get driving or domestic work, in their home offices, on the Internet through tools like Slack—and meet them regardless of their classification, income, or the kind of work they do. To build the mutualist future, the job of the labor movement will be to organize and support all workers.

But how?

Don't Wait for Permission: Experiment, Iterate, Repeat

One of my professors at the Cornell University International School of Industrial and Labor Relations, Clete Daniel, taught me to see the difference between unions and the labor movement as a whole:

- Unions are institutions certified as collective bargaining agents by the government through the Wagner Act.
- The labor movement is a vast and ever-changing social movement dedicated to the uplift of workers that includes all types of strategies deployed by all types of institutions for all types of people: young and old, radical and conservative, professional and low-wage worker.

Unions as we recognize them today are one part of the labor movement—perhaps the most important part. But the labor movement itself is far bigger and older.

One of my favorite stories from the early labor movement is of how John L. Lewis, who rose from the coal mines to the presidency of the United Mine Workers of America, unionized America's coal miners in 1933. Scattered throughout the mountains of Appalachia, miners in West Virginia and Kentucky had never been organized before. To unionize them, Lewis didn't have a national strategy. He didn't have a list of best practices. What he did have, however, was an active base of mine workers, a car, and a big mouth. He drove around Appalachian coal country and said to the coal miners he met along the way: *The president wants you to join the union!* Within three months, Lewis had succeeded in unionizing 92 percent of the country's coal-mining workforce.

I love this story because it's easy to look back at the early labor movement and see the straight line of history pointing toward today. But the truth is that at the time, many leaders and workers were just experimenting, and they disagreed about basic philosophical questions: Who should be in a union? What should a union do? How could they start one? What worked? What didn't? Rather than wait for answers, early labor leaders just tried things to see what worked. The result was a Cambrian explosion of new mutualist activity. Unions like the ILGWU, Amalgamated Clothing Workers of America, and Brotherhood of Sleeping Car Porters laid the groundwork for America's early safety net in the decades before the New Deal.

The same thing is happening now. Today's best labor leaders and worker-activists are rewriting the rules for how to organize workers and defining what a labor union can and should be. This kind of experimentation is happening across the spectrum of work, from blue-collar taxi drivers to white-collar writers and coders. Labor leaders and organizers are looking at this new generation of workers—a generation largely left out of the original legal structures of organized labor and more disparate, divided, and exposed than ever before—and are meeting them where they are. Leaders might disagree about tactics and strategies, but they share a common goal: to improve workers' lives, no matter who they are.

The safety net of the mutualist future will rest on worker-built institutions that are willing to experiment—that just start solving problems and see what works. I already see a number of new unions doing this.

The New York Taxi Workers Alliance—an organization that was founded in 1998 and currently represents 21,000 New York City taxi and for-hire vehicle drivers—may not be the biggest new union and may not be in the forefront of new digital approaches to organizing. But it is anything but a niche organization. Its leaders are bravely and boldly organizing the new workforce no matter what the law says. For more than twenty years, this group has been collecting dues, supporting drivers' strikes, and negotiating with the City of New York for a host of regulatory changes—including winning a cap on the number of Uber and Lyft drivers on the streets of New York, the very change Doug Schifter despaired of ever happening. It is one of the only organizations of independent contractors ever to affiliate with the AFL-CIO, and though the government still doesn't categorize it as a union, this affiliation helps legitimize the plight of underpaid and vulnerable independent contractors in the eyes of the labor movement.

"From the beginning, we've always called ourselves a union, no matter what the law says," Bhairavi Desai, the executive director of the alliance, said at the time it joined the

AFL-CIO. "Affiliating with the AFL-CIO sends the signal that our labor is to be respected. It opens the door to millions of other workers like us."

Similarly, Rideshare Drivers United, a union that represents Uber and Lyft drivers, was started in 2018 on the heels of a drivers' strike at Los Angeles International Airport. As with the Taxi Workers Alliance, the government doesn't formally recognize Rideshare Drivers United as a union. But that hasn't stopped the organization from calling itself an "Uber & Lyft Drivers Union" and using new technologies to unite workers in ways that wouldn't have been possible until recently. It is taking a sophisticated approach to finding today's isolated, app-enabled workers where they already are: on their phones. The organization communicates directly with its members via an app, which it uses to ask them questions (for example, "What is a reasonable commission on a passenger payment for Uber & Lyft to take?: 5%, 10%, 15%, 20%, 25%") or help them navigate the byzantine terms of their work contracts with Uber or Lyft (for example, by sending them a link that allows them to opt out of a Lyft mandatory-arbitration clause, which would prevent them from joining class action lawsuits against the company). Rideshare Drivers United is helping workers make sense of questions about their pay, legal issues, and organizing strategy—questions that workers have looked to their unions to answer in the past. But it is adapting how it communicates those answers to the structure of its members' work. In the absence of the proverbial company watercooler or a physical meeting space, the app makes organizing and communicating with the geographically dispersed and isolated drivers possible. As a consequence, Rideshare Drivers United has been able to pull off a number of large-scale strikes throughout the Los Angeles area and beyond, has protested at California governor Gavin Newsom's office for changes in legislation, has articulated a "Drivers Bill of Rights," which Rideshare is fighting to see reflected in California law, and is helping drivers understand and protect their legal rights.

A freelancer once asked me how he could start a union for book editors. He wanted to know what government department or official he'd need to talk to in order to certify the union, as though starting a union was something you did via application. He was basically asking me how to get *permission* to start a union. It's a common misconception: today's workers are daunted by the formalities of organizing because they feel as though they need professional help to navigate its complexities, and the anti-union changes since Taft-Hartley have only made the process more complex.

But let me be clear: no one needs to give you permission, and there is no one right way to unionize. Today's labor leaders are not waiting to be told the right way to organize workers. They are just out there doing it. You don't need to wait either. Find your community, listen to their problems, and get started. As an independent contractor who has many employers, you may have no "official" way to unionize, and your "union" may not have protection under the Wagner Act, but neither did any union before 1935—and that didn't stop them from organizing and winning real changes.

Use Technology as a Tool

Groups like Rideshare Drivers United are part of what I call the growing trend of *network unionism:* groups of workers organized through social networks who use technology to put those networks to work in new ways. Many of today's most dynamic new labor organizations are part of this trend. Some of them don't call themselves labor organizations at all. And, like the unions on the cutting edge of organizing taxi and rideshare drivers, they aren't waiting for permission or recognition to get started.

Consider Study Hall, a new type of for-profit organization that has created an infrastructure around a collective of a few thousand writers, podcasters, and other media professionals. The organization is deceptively simple: it's structured primarily around an email listserv. But the listserv serves a vibrant and engaged community that ranges from aspiring freelancers trying to get their first byline to established professionals at the top of their field. Members pay a small monthly subscription fee to be a part of Study Hall and can choose different tiers of membership. Access to the listserv alone can cost as little as $1 per month. For a higher fee, members can get access to a range of other resources, including a constellation of Google documents with information like which magazine editors to pitch and how to hone ideas; a digest of job opportunities; and a Slack work space where they can brainstorm about topics such as how to improve their skills, how to get access to training, who pays on time, which employers to avoid, and practical ideas on weathering crises.

Study Hall is a robust network of professionals who are having conversations like those that would have taken place in the best trade unions of the last century. In other words, some of the most important conversations about work are now taking place outside of the workplace, and outside of traditional labor organizations altogether, enabled by technologies that have made it easier than ever to organize workers who don't share a physical place of work.

In addition to worker organizations like Study Hall with public-facing names, there are also private, invitation-only groups geared toward small groups of professional freelancers at the top of their field. These include a Google Group of former book publishing employees who now make up most of the freelance workforce whose expertise supports the ever-dwindling full-time staff at major publishing houses, and the women-only Binders Facebook group for writers, which at one point was said to have more than 31,000 members. There are nonprofits like Coworker.org, which helps workers at a range of different employers petition for change. It was behind an organized walkout of Google workers in 2018 and helped workers at Starbucks win changes like getting parental leave policies extended to include fathers and adoptive parents. There are networks of Silicon Valley tech talent, like the Tech Workers Coalition and Silicon Valley Rising. The National Domestic Workers Alliance is an advocacy powerhouse that has successfully organized domestic workers, who are also excluded from the New Deal safety net, and has been winning policy victories on their behalf since 2007. These new unions may not be recognized as such by the government under the Wagner Act, but in terms of their mission and their goals, they are no different from the guilds of the 1800s, the industrial workers' unions of the 1930s, or the public sector teachers who leveraged social media to build a critical mass for strikes in a number of states, including West Virginia, in 2018.

But technology is just a tool. It can help scale new forms of worker organizations, but it is no replacement for the basic principle that organizing has to start with the real needs of workers. Importantly, tomorrow's labor movement must recognize that those needs have changed.

Listen to the Real Needs of Workers

Both traditional unions and new freelancer-focused organizations have a role to play in organizing tomorrow's workforce. When industrial unions burst onto the scene during the rise of industrialization, craft unions didn't disappear. Instead, both kinds of unions were needed. Likewise today, writers enjoy protections from both the National Writers Union, which has been organizing writers as independent contractors since 1981, and the Writers Guild of America, which has its roots in 1930s-era Hollywood and has been organizing New York City newsrooms—where writers are full-time employees, which means they can be organized under the labor laws that already exist—for decades. Recently they helped workers at the now defunct online media company and blog network Gawker unionize. In the following years a number of other online newsrooms followed suit by unionizing, either through the Writers Guild or another union, the NewsGuild, most notably at Vice Media, Salon, *Slate*, The Onion, The Huffington Post, BuzzFeed, and Gimlet. There is a place for organizing both employees and independent contractors in today's workplace.

But that's not the whole story. Consider the debate around worker "misclassification." Some traditional unions—unions that are operating within the New Deal's framework—try to organize independent contractors by arguing that they are actually "misclassified" employees. The "misclassification" argument is most frequently invoked in conversations about companies like Uber and Lyft, which insist that their drivers don't work for them. "Drivers' work is outside the usual course of Uber's business," Uber's legal counsel has said, "which is serving as a technology platform for several different types of digital marketplaces." Of course, this is absurd: many drivers rely entirely on Uber or Lyft for their livelihoods. In this case, these workers probably are misclassified employees.

But other parts of today's independent workforce simply don't fit the old manufacturing-era model framed by the Wagner Act. More than half of all freelancers say that no amount of money would get them to switch back to a traditional job. They're not misclassified employees; they are true independent contractors. Not only do most freelancers not have an obvious would-be employer who is misclassifying them, but for many of them, the freedom, flexibility, and ownership they get from freelancing is of the essence.

By misunderstanding the real needs of workers, we run the risk of unwittingly committing the cardinal sin against the labor movement: pitting workers against one another. Advocates of policies that address misclassification inadvertently turn freelancing into a wedge issue: politicians on the left have accused true freelancers of being anti-labor, while politicians on the right have portrayed such pro-worker policies as being out of touch with the way work really happens today.

The U.S. House of Representatives recently passed the Protecting the Right to Organize (PRO) Act, a much-needed update to existing labor laws that, among other things, aims to address the problem of worker misclassification. Legislation against misclassification addresses a real problem—that is, that today's workforce lacks a safety net—but the danger is that such legislation may be written so broadly that it will hurt the very workers it is intended to protect. True independent contractors are an enormous and expanding portion of our nation's workforce, and legislation that treats these freelancers as misclassified employees doesn't take into account how they really work. These workers chose to be freelancers, and they value the flexibility that freelancing offers. They need a safety net that works for them rather than one that tries to shoehorn them into yesterday's New Deal framework—a safety net that makes issues like "misclassification" irrelevant because it views all workers the same way: as deserving of protections.

This means recognizing the legitimacy of today's new unions, which are meeting workers where they are, regardless of their classification. But the challenge these unions face isn't just that the government doesn't formally recognize them as unions. It's also that because they are not recognized as unions, they have no regulatory framework in which to fund themselves. Traditional unions can justify charging dues because collective bargaining is such a valuable service. By contrast, without being able to provide services with real economic value to their members, these new unions can't charge the kinds of dues that would allow them to build the self-sustaining social institutions workers need—institutions capable of developing real bargaining power in today's economy.

Political Power Comes from Economic Power, or Thank God We Sell Insurance

When we were building support for the Freelancers Union model of portable benefits, we organized a members meeting with the most significant New York State leader who could support us at the time: Sheldon Silver. I still remember it as being one of the most unlikely meetings I've ever been a part of. At a dive bar on the Lower East Side, we brought a group of young, tattooed and pierced independent freelancers—creatives from across industries—together with Silver, an Orthodox Jew, who at the time was the Speaker of the New York State Assembly. My goal was for Silver to hear directly from these freelancers how much they valued buying their insurance through the Freelancers Union, in the hope that he would be an advocate for us in the assembly. Like any good union, our goal was to demonstrate to Silver that we were building the support of freelancers in his district, and that they knew he was a champion of the affordable, portable benefits they got through Freelancers Union. It was a great meeting.

My mantra at the Freelancers Union was "Thank God we sell insurance." Because we had a financial base, we had staying power, and once we saw exactly how government could be helpful to our freelancers, we could articulate our freelancers' needs to government. The New York State government listened to us and helped us innovate by adapting regulations that enabled us to use our revenues to make a meaningful difference in our members' lives. And most important, our revenues helped us be independent: we could say "no" to funding streams that weren't a fit for our freelancers. Without a financial base, we would have had no such leverage.

New unions like Rideshare Drivers United are able to organize large numbers of workers, but without a sustainable business model, they run the risk of ending up like the Knights of Labor in the late nineteenth century, which burned brightly and briefly but failed to survive over the long term. Tomorrow's unions need to find a way to become both economically self-sustaining and independent.

Take the Independent Drivers Guild, for example, an organization similar to Rideshare Drivers United. The Guild has real trade union bona fides and, like the New York Taxi Workers Alliance, is connected to the AFL-CIO (in the Guild's case, through its relationship with the International Association of Machinists and Aerospace Workers). The Independent Drivers Guild had the same challenge that all new unions face: without being able to collectively bargain on behalf of its members, it couldn't charge sustainable dues. So the Guild partnered with Uber itself, which today contributes part of the Guild's revenue. Critics hold that the Independent Drivers Guild is really just a "company union"—a kind of employer-sponsored union made illegal by the New Deal—and as such is an opportunity for Uber to give the appearance of working with a labor organization while actually tightly controlling the nature and magnitude of the concessions it chooses to give. There's some truth to that, but with Uber's funding, the Independent Drivers Guild has been able to build a real organization that has delivered real gains to its members. Still, without the protection of the Wagner Act to help them self-fund, organizations like the Guild are in a tough position. I sympathize: when I was at the Freelancers Union and we couldn't get foundation support to continue our work on portable benefits, we partnered with Uber as well.

Until today's new labor organizations can become economically self-sustaining, they're never going to be truly independent. And as long as they have to rely largely on companies like Uber or charitable foundations for the core of their financial stability, they will never achieve the kind of independence, longevity, or self-sustaining power that strong mutualist organizations need. But if we could give these new unions a sustainable economic mechanism, they could do so much more. Company unions started in the 1920s by the American Telephone and Telegraph Company (later re-branded as AT&T) eventually evolved into the Communications Workers of America, a union that today boasts close to 700,000 members, supported Democratic candidate Bernie Sanders's bid for the presidency in 2016, and through its affiliate the NewsGuild helped organize many of the newsrooms discussed earlier in this chapter.

These new unions need help. Franklin Roosevelt gave unions a "job"—collective bargaining for higher wages—and state and local governments need to do the same for today's, and tomorrow's, unions as well. They could do that by passing legislation and changing regulations to enable the unions to offer services of real value to their members, such as providing insurance, retirement, and job training. This isn't a one-size-fits-all strategy—after all, mutualist communities are different, and their needs are, too—but if mutualist organizations that hold economic power can engage government in conversations about their most pressing needs, the next safety net will begin to make itself.

"The blue-collar blues is no more bitterly sung than the white-collar moan," Studs Terkel wrote in 1974, in the introduction to his book *Working*. From the front seats of taxicabs to the newsrooms of BuzzFeed and the open-office floor plans of Google, today's new workforce deserves a voice. To meet its needs, labor leaders need to find them where they are and organize them in a way that addresses their day-to-day realities.

Silicon Valley is building innovative technologies that are transforming the economy we grew up with. I'm looking to the new unions—the ones that are already being equally innovative in building new structures and strategies to deal with the new economy head-on—to be the future of the labor movement. Workers deserve to organize themselves, full stop, and these new unions are taking the first steps toward offering them a chance to do so, regardless of their status, their income, or the nature of their work. These workers are building the institutions they need, and the labor movement needs to stand behind what they build. What's most important today is reminding those workers who feel the most isolated from one another that they are not alone, and that when they stand together, they do indeed have a voice.

Just as the guilds of the pre-industrial era led to the formation of craft unions and, eventually, industrial unions, so, too, will the organizations that are forming around workers today lay the groundwork for the next era's network unions. The unions of tomorrow will be part of a reemergent solidarity in America—the builders and the experimentalists who will rebuild the next economy from the ground up. Some of these organizations will fail, others will succeed; some will be legislated out of existence, others will be protected. It's impossible to know which will be which. The important thing is that workers are experimenting, organizing themselves, and seeing what works.

New kinds of unions have always arisen to meet the challenges of a new era because workers always find one another and begin to build the institutions they need. It's happening again now. Next, we need to change the rules of government and capital to give these unions—as well as the cooperatives, mutual aid societies, religious organizations, and other mutualist groups—the tools to build the power they need to scale. As they grow, they'll in turn transform the economy to put human beings, and the planet, at its center.

CHAPTER 8

The Future of Government

Give Mutualists a Job

Government's role in the mutualist future will be to define the mutualist sector, and to pivot toward scaling that sector by creating a market that lets it thrive. By recognizing the role that religious organizations, mutual aid societies, cooperatives, and unions already play in helping local communities meet their needs, and by putting a regulatory structure around these organizations, government will give the mutualist sector a "job" in the new economy. That job will transform our notion of what a safety net can be in the twenty-first century: place-based, responsive to the environment, gentle on the body and mind—in short, a safety net that will encourage people to connect as a way to thrive. Governments of the future will be measured by the degree to which they help the mutualist sector grow.

In November of 2019, *The New York Times* reported on a promising mutualist trend: the growing prevalence of worker-owned cooperative grocery stores that deliver fresh, healthy, affordable produce and groceries to communities in parts of rural America where low-cost retail chains like Dollar General have driven traditional grocery stores out of business. These cooperatives are a way for communities to take responsibility for their own future. "People around here haven't spent a lot of time around co-ops in the city," a lawyer who opened one such store in Winchester, Illinois, said. "We just sold it from straight novelty. Our way was playing off local sentiment—this isn't charity. This was self-responsibility. If you want a grocery store in town, you have to step up." And step up they did.

These new local cooperative solutions to affordable groceries are one-offs, born of necessity. But if government fully supported mutualists with public policy and access to capital, you might find such cooperative solutions to the problems of daily life woven into the very fabric of society. In Emilia-Romagna, cooperative utilities, housing cooperatives, farmers cooperatives, cooperatively owned manufacturing, cooperative healthcare, cooperative elder care, and cooperative care for the disabled are how citizens today get their basic needs met. The result is that they have access to good food, well-paying jobs, insurance, affordable housing, and security as they age.

This is the power that government can have in creating the next safety net. A comprehensive plan to build up the mutualist sector could produce something similar to Emilia-Romagna here in America. Communities like Winchester, Illinois, might build more than just cooperative grocery stores; they might build cooperative elder care, cooperative job training, and more.

To become economically self-sustaining mutualist enterprises with a job in the new economy, local mutualists need government support. To help them grow into self-sustaining institutions capable of delivering tomorrow's safety net, government can build up the mutualist sector in a number of ways.

> First, recognize and define mutualism as a sector of the economy unto itself—a sector that has already begun to deliver the next safety net.

> Second, use the tools at its disposal (the tax code and other regulations) to create a market for mutualist economic activity—in effect, by giving these mutualist organizations a job.

> Third, protect, rather than replace, the mutualist solutions to social problems that already exist.

Recognize the Mutualist Sector

Government has offered comprehensive support and protection to parts of the mutualist sector before. The First Amendment to our Constitution created the right of religious freedom, a top priority for early Americans, and the separation of church and state has been a hallowed principle of American life ever since. Religious organizations have used that protection to build a gigantic base of economic and political power, and tax exemptions have allowed them to keep their capital away from the pressures of the traditional marketplace to do what they do best: form communities locally and put an economic infrastructure around those communities. This work has included building hospitals, schools, universities, hospices, orphanages, and more. By using a wide array of policy tools to protect religious organizations as a sector, government can enable them to make a meaningful difference in their communities.

Regulations and the tax code have been used in other ways, too. The boom in cooperative housing built by unions in the early part of the twentieth century was facilitated by a series of laws offering tax exemptions and limitations on rents that created the right economic conditions for unions like the Amalgamated Clothing Workers of America to enter the housing market. In 1974, the Employee Retirement Income Security Act created employee stock ownership plans (ESOPs), which give tax advantages to companies that offer their employees an equity stake in the company as a whole. And as recently as the 1990s, the government even put its muscle behind a younger kind of mutualist organization: community development financial institutions (CDFIs), through the CDFI Fund. These institutions, which have their origins in the 1970s and the Community Reinvestment Act, serve the interests of local communities, especially poorer communities, before they serve a profit goal. Today, New York State alone has more than eighty CDFIs, which range from the crunchy Alternatives Federal Credit Union in Ithaca to Carver Federal Savings Bank (named after George Washington Carver), a Harlem-based bank founded in 1948 that was at one time the largest Black-owned-and-operated financial institution in the country.

Government has supported mutualist activity again and again throughout our country's history, but it has never done so consistently or systematically. Progressive regulatory policy and forward-thinking leadership occasionally align to create circumstances that produce meaningful mutualist activity where it didn't exist before, but these favorable circumstances are almost always temporary, accidental, exceptional, or just plain lucky. What if, instead, government had a systematic strategy for supporting mutualist organizations? Most of these organizations already qualify for nonprofit status, but what if we intentionally created the right conditions for mutualism to scale through the tax and regulatory code? What if there was a political constituency dedicated to winning the votes to make it happen?

To do that, first government will have to recognize that mutualism is a sector unto itself worth protecting, so that it can bring its alphabet soup of tools to bear on supporting it. Once we define the mutualist sector, government and voters alike will see it for what it already is: a massive part of the country's economy that serves a huge constituency and really does change people's lives.

Create a Market for Mutualism: Give It a Job

Defining the sector is the first step. Next, government will need to create a capital market in which mutualism can thrive.

When I started the Freelancers Union, I knew that we needed to find a job for ourselves: a sustainable economic mechanism that would give us enough of a return to allow us to build a lasting institution for our community. Since we represented freelancers—independent contractors with numerous employers—charging dues in exchange for collective bargaining wasn't an option. Our solution—the job we gave ourselves—was to provide health insurance and other benefits to our community of freelancers. This business model was key to our viability.

But we also owe the early success of the Freelancers Union's insurance businesses to the fact that the State of New York created a regulatory pathway that allowed us to group all of our freelancers together, putting us in an actuarial category that let us design and price plans as though freelancers were one large group, like a big corporation. This category, designated "M" for miscellaneous, created a market for us to exist in, as well as a huge pathway for growth that enabled us to expand from a brokerage to the Freelancers Insurance Company. For years, this meant that freelancers had access to the kind of quality health insurance that was usually available only to employees at big corporations. The regulatory designation gave us a job—to provide benefits to freelancers—which enabled us to build an entire ecosystem in New York State around freelancers, modeled on the way Sidney Hillman used the Amalgamated union as a base to build an ecosystem around clothing workers.

This is not unlike how Franklin Roosevelt used the Wagner Act to create a market for the unions of his day to exist. By protecting these unions' right to engage in collective bargaining, he gave them a mandate to pursue activities of real value to workers and to become self-sustaining mutualist institutions that could protect the workers they represented. Government gave unions—nonprofits with regulatory exemptions from antitrust laws and insurance regulations typically available only to large employers—the legal, regulatory, and tax-exempt status that let them thrive. Government will need to do the same thing for the entire mutualist sector in the future: define them and create a market for their economic activity.

How? Government has always created, destroyed, regulated, and preferred markets through the tools at its disposal.

There's no reason it can't deploy these tools instead to support a diverse ecosystem of mutualist organizations. Rather than waiting for mutualist activity to spring up organically, as we have in the past, government could provide all kinds of support to mutualist organizations to facilitate and encourage their growth: refundable tax credits, low-interest loans, use of government spaces, zoning assistance, and more.

To help mutualist organizations get off the ground, government could offer tax breaks for individuals, corporations, banks, and other financial institutions that donate to or invest in mutualism. We already do this for foundations and nonprofits, which collectively have revenues of more than $2 trillion today. Government already requires foundations with endowments to distribute 5 percent of their returns to charity. What if we required foundations to earmark an additional amount—call it just 1 percent of the returns on their endowments—to fund mutualist organizations in the broader community?

We could ask the same of venture capital firms, which often get their own money from pools of capital that have been mutualistically gathered, like university endowments and pension funds, especially unionized pension funds. What if the tax code required that they give a little of their profits, say 1 percent, back to the capital markets they pull from by investing in mutualist organizations?

After the 2007–2008 financial crisis, the Federal Reserve injected a huge amount of money into the economy by purchasing toxic assets from banks in a process called quantitative easing. Unlike traditional banks, the Federal Reserve is a patient investor that had a mission to remove these toxic assets from banks to make them sturdier when they were at their most precarious. These patient investments became hugely profitable over the following eight years, and that profit, like all profits earned by the Fed, went back into the U.S. Treasury and then right over to Congress. If we had earmarked even a tiny percentage of it for investment in new mutualist organizations, we could have actually accomplished something with it: built a pool of mutualist capital to fix the food supply chain, deliver healthcare during a public health crisis, address the opioid epidemic, or repair aging infrastructure, for example.

Government could even borrow an idea from Emilia-Romagna and create our own American notion of indivisible reserves: profits that aren't taxed, but that are required to be reinvested in new mutualist organizations. State and local government's economic development funds and sovereign wealth funds are other examples of pools of money that government has at its disposal. Earmarking even a tiny portion of this money to invest in mutualism would create an enormous new market for mutualist organizations.

However we do it, the point is that existing pools of large capital could be repurposed to build a market for mutualism. The aggregate effect of policies like these would be to create something that new mutualist organizations need to get off the ground but that is largely absent in 2021: new patient capital markets. These existing pools of money could help fund new mutualist businesses by giving them access to meaningful amounts of capital, but at rates that would let them put their social purpose ahead of profits. A government mandate for mutualist economic activity through the creation of these markets would let today's proto-mutualist organizations—like Rideshare Drivers United and Study Hall—take their economic activity to the next level: to become powerful economic engines that form the cornerstone

of communities and become increasingly complex and sophisticated parts of their members' lives. In short, it would
give them a job.

Protect Mutualist Gems

Mutualist solutions work best when government recognizes,
supports, and facilitates the growth of mutualist solutions in
local communities, and when it tries to engage them in a
conversation about how their needs can be met over time.
When it tries to replace them wholesale, organizations that
have been meeting a local need in a targeted, effective way—
mutualist gems—are wiped off the map.

This happened to me. It was 2008, and we at the burgeoning Freelancers Insurance Company weren't the only
people aware that there was a healthcare crisis in progress.
Senator Barack Obama had campaigned for president on a
platform of healthcare reform, and when he took office, he
promptly got to work on the passage of a bill intended to
lower the barriers to and the costs of getting high-quality
healthcare to as many Americans as possible. In March of
2010, the Affordable Care Act (ACA) was written into law.

It was a goal I certainly shared. After all, I had spent years
tuning the Freelancers Union and the Freelancers Insurance
Company's insurance product to meet the needs of freelancers. But although Senator Ted Kennedy's staff worked to ensure that our model was protected under the new act, in the
end the ACA's path through Congress was complicated and
delicate, and by the time the law took effect in 2014 our solution was too small to be a priority. Our "M" designation,
which had created a market for us to exist, was taken away,

and we were left out of the new law entirely. Although most of our investors were sympathetic to what was happening— one of them, the head of Prudential's impact investing program, Ommeed Sathe, told me later, "If you get hit by an asteroid, you get hit by an asteroid; you don't blame the tyrannosaurus for not seeing it coming"—we were devastated.

So were our members. In our last quarter, when our outgoing customers were finally able to log on to the New York State of Health marketplace and see what their new insurance was going to look like under the ACA, they began to see how special our experiment in mutualist healthcare had been. Buying insurance in the ACA's individual marketplace was great for lower-income freelancers who qualified for significant subsidies. But for higher-paid workers who were just above the subsidy levels, the change meant that their coverage was about to shrink, their premiums were about to go up, and the quality of their care was about to go down. In New York State, out-of-network insurance was gone entirely for individuals at that time, meaning that the doctors they had seen for years were no longer available to them. In the Freelancers Insurance Company's last three months, our members spent $12 million on healthcare plans that were about to vanish: a mad dash to take advantage of quality insurance before it was gone. To the legislators focused on passing the ACA, we were just a small insurance company that happened to be really good at cost containment. They missed the fact that we were also a deeply rooted mutualist ecosystem that extended beyond insurance into the very livelihoods of our freelancers. Our mutualist strategy was invisible to the government. As a consequence, so were we.

When the Culinary Workers Union in Nevada took a stand against nationalized health insurance during the

2020 presidential primary, saying they preferred the health plan they got through their union, I couldn't help but be reminded of my own experience at the Freelancers Insurance Company. What proposals for nationalized health plans miss is this: the Culinary Workers Union health plan, negotiated over the course of decades, has served 130,000 union members and their families so well that they were willing to choose their presidential candidate based on it. Solutions like this are worth protecting as part of the wider mutualist sector. Nonetheless, it was de rigueur for many progressives at the time to support a nationalized health plan instead of listening to workers' voices. The idea that a small-scale, progressive solution to healthcare that made sense for tens of thousands of workers was simply an inconvenience to be ignored in favor of a large-scale, top-down government solution, rather than at the very least a strategy to be understood and perhaps even emulated, comes out of a frame of reference I've seen too often: that government is the only institution capable of driving real social change at scale.

There's no reason that proposals for nationalized healthcare can't coexist with mutualism, but mutualist organizations themselves—unions, cooperatives, mutual aid societies, faith communities—are uniquely positioned to be the delivery mechanism for that care. Giving mutualists the job of building a safety net tuned to the needs of their own communities would change all of our experiences of our daily lives. In contrast to a uniform set of corporate benefits, such a safety net would be a return to the original roots of healthcare, insurance, and housing—all of which were originally designed by the mutualist sector to be locally based, sensitive to communities, and human in scale.

Change the Frame

While Republicans since Ronald Reagan have made it clear that they do not want an activist government, many of today's progressive leaders likewise miss the fact that government is most effective when it supports mutualist activity that is already taking place. Today's progressive leaders too often look only to government for solutions to today's social problems, and thus ignore how social problems have actually been solved throughout American history. Local organizations themselves are the economic drivers that need to be scaled. By creating a market for a new mutualist sector, government could encourage the growth of mutualist organizations on a scale big enough to tackle some of our toughest problems. Government must give mutualist organizations the tools they need to thrive, get out of the way and let them grow, and support them as they mature into mutualist ecosystems.

We need a new politics, one that goes beyond the monolithic government solutions of the left and the free market, libertarian individualism of the right to recognize the community solutions that have always filled in the gaps. Today, as we are living through an era of extreme government dysfunction, we have to start building the future we need. We can start in our local communities. And when we succeed, we'll have built up the political and economic base enough to get government to notice. To achieve the kind of progressive change America needs, our government leaders must recognize just how profoundly the world has changed and acknowledge that the mutualist sector already has many of the answers. To become a useful partner to mutualism, government must enshrine, protect, and grow the mutualist sector by building new kinds of capital markets—the patient capital markets that will allow mutualism to flourish.

CHAPTER 9

The Future of Capital

A Market for Mutualism

When we started the Freelancers Insurance Company in 2008, we were lucky. We needed access to patient capital, and we found it. A few foundations understood our strategy and were interested in building new benefits models for freelancers, and we were able to qualify for a form of foundation-backed debt called program-related investment (PRI), which we could repay in ten years with low interest rates of 1 or 2 percent. As we built the Freelancers Union's economic model, we raised several rounds of foundation funding, eventually securing $17 million to get the union's most significant effort off the ground. With this patient capital in hand, we could start practicing mutualism right away.

Years later, in 2017, I tried to do the same thing again when I started a new benefits platform for freelancers called Trupo. When I started talking to investors, I heard the same thing again and again: this is a great idea, but it won't work as a nonprofit. They would invest only if we ran the company in a way they could recognize: as a for-profit startup, with the goals of scale and quick returns that the traditional startup model entails. As a result, I became the CEO of an insurtech startup, only my second job at a for-profit company in my life. (My first was when I worked at a department store in high school.)

Why did I become the CEO of a for-profit startup? Because today there are very few patient capital markets available to social entrepreneurs who want to scale their ideas. Capital markets—pools of money that help entrepreneurs get things done—fall into three major categories: charitable, mutualist (or patient), and fast. We have a few types of charitable funding—foundation grants, for example—and a wide range of fast capital funding, from venture capital to private equity to impact investing. But between these two is the mutualist category, in which there is no consistent patient lending source for social purpose entrepreneurs.

Why do we need patient capital markets? Like all businesses, mutualist organizations need investments of capital to get off the ground, to be sustainable while they grow, and ultimately to scale. But unlike conventional businesses, mutualist organizations reinvest profits into their communities rather than pursue outsized returns to pay their investors. These organizations need lenders who recognize that while they'll ultimately make money, their investments are first and foremost intended to help a community solve a social problem. Without these patient investments, mutualist entrepreneurs are left to decide between taking charity and putting profits over the needs of their communities.

How can we fix this? As we saw in chapter 8, government can help create the right market conditions for patient lending to occur by changing the tax code, earmarking money for mutualist enterprises in state and local development budgets, and offering tax deductions for investment in mutualist organizations.

But entrepreneurs and investors will also have to use these new patient capital markets to direct the flow of capital away from the pockets of shareholders and into the hands of communities. They can do this by recycling a percentage of the profits from investments made by endowments and unionized pension funds (both examples of capital gathered mutualistically) back into the mutualist sector, by changing their ideas about what profits are for, and by training tomorrow's patient capitalists.

I recently asked Ommeed Sathe, one of the investors who backed the Freelancers Insurance Company, why there are so few patient capital markets today. "At a very high level," he said, "people understand what philanthropy is, and they understand what investing is. Both have a clarity and unanimity of perspective. As most things in life, things that are in between are hard for people to understand—and they're really hard for people to institutionalize. To me the North Star is not 'Can you get capital to do something crazy and irrational once?' It's 'Can you get capital to change the direction of the river?'"

Imagine if it was as clear a pathway to get money to start a cooperative grocery or to create reserves to turn your Google Group of fellow freelancers into a digital mutual aid society that could offer its members mutual unemployment insurance as it is to get a mortgage or apply for a credit card. Imagine if there was ready funding available to start a cooperative daycare with other parents in your community. Or if it was just as easy for an entrepreneur to get money to build a new, low-cost, freelancer-focused mutual insurance company that was designed to serve you as it is for entrepreneurs to get money to scale for-profit startups designed to make their investors rich.

To close the gap between the world we live in and the world I envision—a world in which money is accessible and flows easily to real social entrepreneurs who want to solve a problem for their community—we need to change the direction of the river of capital. To do that, there are steps tomorrow's mutualist entrepreneurs will need to take.

First, invest in and replenish the mutualist sector—diminished today, but strong not so long ago.

Second, change their frame from an extractive lending model to a lending model that facilitates recycling capital back into communities.

Third, train tomorrow's mutualist entrepreneurs.

Fourth, invest in and build group infrastructure to scale the mutualist future.

Invest in the Mutualist Sector

It hasn't always been this way. The mutualist sector of our economy, still a robust and thriving economic force in its own right, hasn't been replenished in decades. But the institutions that mutualist entrepreneurs built in the last period of mutualist innovation are still with us.

Amalgamated Bank, which today manages $40 billion in assets, helped finance some of the earliest experiments in co-operative housing by making small loans, with little collateral and low interest rates, to working people who couldn't qualify for loans at traditional banks. The result of this patient lending, the Amalgamated Housing Cooperative, was built in 1927 and still stands in the Bronx today. A wave of cooperative housing all across New York City followed, including housing sponsored by my own family's ILGWU: the East River Housing Corporation, part of Cooperative Village; Penn South in Chelsea; and, decades later, Rochdale Village and Electchester in Queens (conceived by Harry Van Arsdale, Jr., the leader of the International Brotherhood of Electrical Workers). These housing cooperatives were able to keep the use of real estate as a fast capital investment vehicle to a minimum by restricting members' ability to resell their shares in the co-op. As a result, many New Yorkers can still buy into the cooperative housing sector today.

The early 1920s also saw the formation of a number cooperative enterprises that we may recognize by name, though we might be surprised to learn that they're cooperatives: Ace Hardware, which was founded in 1924 when four Chicago hardware store owners realized they could get better prices for stock if they pooled their resources and bought items sold in their stores as a group; Land O'Lakes, which dates back to 1921, when 320 Minnesota dairy farmers convened in St. Paul and voted to start the Minnesota Cooperative Creameries Association; grocery stores like IGA and ShopRite, hardware stores like Do it Best and True Value, and even hotel chains like Best Western, which all operate under similar cooperative models (some of these date back to the 1920s, others to the postwar boom of the 1940s). There are even cooperative sports franchises: the Green Bay Packers, which was founded in 1923 when its original owners sold shares to members of the Green Bay community for a couple of dollars apiece. Today, the Packers are the only nonprofit, publicly owned sports franchise in the United States: 361,311 individuals collectively own more than 5 million shares in the Packers.

Cooperatives are how much of the United States gets basic utilities like electricity, especially in rural areas of the country. The Roanoke Electric Cooperative in North Carolina, for instance, was founded in 1938 thanks to the Rural Electrification Act, a piece of legislation signed by Franklin Roosevelt in 1936 that promoted the creation of electrical cooperatives to fund the construction of electricity lines throughout rural America. The Roanoke Electric Cooperative turned on its first power lines in 1939 with 317 member-owners. Today, it serves 14,500 member-owners in seven counties in rural North Carolina. Similar utility cooperatives exist all over the United States.

But since these mutualist organizations were formed, the rules of capital have increasingly favored bigger, quicker bets. With little new investment, the mutualist sector has not been replenished for decades. Government deregulation has resulted in turbocharged fast capital markets that have replaced the patient capital markets that allowed these mutualist solutions of the past to grow and thrive.

Instead, venture capitalists are eager to bet on big ideas, and their end goal is to make an equally big profit. They are looking for a tenfold return on their investment in six to ten years. They're looking to invest in companies that will come to dominate their field: Google for search, Uber for transportation, Airbnb for hospitality, SpaceX for space travel. Since these investors know that only a small percentage of the companies they invest in will make money, they need their successes to be huge—the goal from the beginning is homogeneity, not diversity—and their profits go back to the investors, leaving little left over to reinvest into the community the company serves.

Even investors who ostensibly operate with a social purpose still come at it from a profit maximization frame first. When looking for funding for Trupo, I found that impact investors—whose guiding principle is to demonstrate that it's possible to receive the same return on investment as traditional venture capitalists while investing in companies that have a social purpose—are nonetheless still focused on fast-capital-sized returns. They see the purpose of profit the same way venture capitalists do: as something to be maximized and returned to investors rather than as the by-product of a successful social mission that can be recycled back into the community. The same could be said for B Corporations, or B Corps, which prioritize worker well-being, environmental sustainability, community engagement, and other benchmarks, but still put the for-profit company, rather than the community, at the center of their operations. These companies are helping to change the conversation about important social issues, but they're not the same as a dedicated social sector or a community that builds its own organizations from the ground up. These for-profit companies do good, but ultimately they still come at social responsibility from a traditional profit perspective.

To reinvest in mutualism, we need to remember what J. S. Potofsky, vice president of the Amalgamated Clothing Workers of America, said of Amalgamated Bank in the early twentieth century: "Profits are merely the yardstick to denote the successful operation of the bank—a mere byproduct, as it were." Profits are first and foremost for the community a mutualist organization serves.

Recycle Capital, Don't Extract It

Our laws and regulations so favor fast capital that even in the case of mature, established mutualist organizations that have figured out a great business model and succeeded in collecting huge amounts of capital—university endowments, union benefit and pension funds, mutualized insurance—the decisions about how to use that capital have often been taken out of the hands of the organizations themselves. Government regulation requires the boards of these organizations and the professionals who manage their funds to behave as prudent investors, which today has effectively come to mean they have a mandate to maximize returns. The result: organizations that successfully collect capital mutualistically nonetheless don't invest it mutualistically themselves. Instead, they invest in the fast capital markets of venture capital and private equity, and the decisions about how to use the capital collected rest with professional fund managers, not with the communities they serve. While the fund managers may have some latitude here and there to pursue a social goal, it's always within the context of continuing to deliver high returns. This makes sense to some extent: pension funds need sufficient returns to allow their workers to retire, and universities use their endowments to run the institution and offer free or reduced tuition to their students. But we have separated the investment strategy from the social purpose of the funds, and as a result these large pools of capital are used to make a tiny sliver of the wealthiest 1 percent of the financial industry wealthy, not reinvested in other communities that require access to sources of patient capital in order to build the institutions they need.

This is exactly what happened to mutual insurance companies over the past hundred years. These companies would collect a few months' worth of premiums ahead of time and set them aside as "reserves": stockpiles of capital reserved for times when policyholders made more claims than their premiums could cover. When the companies had excess cash, they would first use it to replenish their reserves. A portion of what was left over—that is, the profit—would then be returned to the policyholders.

A great system, right? So what happened to it?

By the late twentieth century, mutual insurance companies were multimillion-dollar enterprises, but with no patient capital markets available to them, they had nowhere to turn other than the private sector if they wanted to scale. During the Reagan years, the financial industry saw huge potential for growth in mutual insurance companies and engaged in a campaign to demutualize much of the insurance industry. Once privatized, these companies had a fiduciary duty to their investors, not their policyholders. As a result, today the industry is so focused on writing insurance policies that will give them the best chance of earning the biggest returns that the policies are now more expensive and cover less, the industry has become allergic to innovation for fear of losing money, and more Americans are left exposed to risk.

Other famous experiments in mutualist lending have been similarly upended by extractive capitalism. For example, Muhammad Yunus pioneered the field of microcredit by starting Grameen Bank in the 1970s and '80s. He built a sustainable business offering small loans to the poor in Bangladesh, based on tight networks of social relationships. He won the Nobel Peace Prize in 2006 for his work in establishing these new lending practices. But his success was complicated by the fact that unscrupulous lenders saw an opportunity in his model and moved in to capitalize on this new market, pursuing aggressive for-profit strategies that preyed on the communities they were meant to serve. "In 1983, I founded Grameen Bank to provide small loans that people, especially poor women, could use to bring themselves out of poverty," Yunus wrote in *The New York Times* in 2011. "At that time, I never imagined that one day microcredit would give rise to its own breed of loan sharks. But it has."

After serving on the boards of the Federal Reserve Bank of New York and the Nathan Cummings Foundation, a progressive family foundation where I learned about endowments, I concluded that there is another way. We need to earmark some of the profits from mutualistically collected funds—unionized pension funds, endowments, insurance reserves—for reinvestment back into the communities the funds actually serve. The fast capitalists who manage these funds circle the globe looking for the most profitable investments. Surely at least some of the profits from those investments could be used to benefit the communities they pull from. It doesn't have to be 50 percent, but neither should it be 1 percent. With even a mere 10 percent earmarked to be reinvested in the mutualist sector, we'd begin to change the flow of capital in America.

Train Tomorrow's Patient Capitalists

As fast capital has hollowed out the mutualist sector of the American economy, we have not just lost organizations that served their communities first. We have also lost the mutualist expertise of the people who ran those organizations. Gone are the staff who really cared about their communities, and the board members who were loyal to the mutualist organizations they came up in. Boards are now filled with professionals dedicated to the mandate of maximum returns. So patient capital markets aren't enough to kick-start the mutualist sector. We also need to repopulate it with the right talent: social entrepreneurs who see capital as a tool—one they can use to accomplish their important social goals.

To a progressive who didn't come up in a mutualist institution and has never experienced the reciprocal economic relationship that occurs inside one, the idea of a patient, progressive capital market might sound like an oxymoron. Many progressives view markets primarily as exploitative and government as the major tool for social change in the progressive tool kit (that and the charitable model, in which rich people donate their money to a favorite cause). But markets are just a basis for exchange, and they can be structured in a number of different ways. Many markets are designed to be extractive. But there's no reason we can't build patient markets—markets designed to help communities get access to affordable groceries, for example—to solve whatever social problems we encounter as well.

But we need people who know how to use them. The foundation world and the venture capital world already have sophisticated pipelines to identify, fund, incubate, and grow the most promising new entrepreneurs, ideas, and talent. Y Combinator, an accelerator that provides seed funding for startups, places a suite of help, training, and assistance around the most promising entrepreneurs, then helps them raise their first round of capital. In the process, Y Combinator becomes a curator of startups in their earliest stages, and the competition to invest in the companies they support is keen. As a society, we've greased the wheels of how startup founders get money from venture capitalists. What if we did the same thing to help mutualist founders get funding into their communities? Since they would be solving problems for their communities, a mutualist incubator would start to look like a cross section of America, full of mutualist leaders who are a reflection of our whole society, tackling problems for their communities with open minds and hearts. The two best models for incubating this kind of new mutualist talent are Ashoka and Echoing Green, which over the past several decades have built up and nurtured robust networks of true social entrepreneurs in America and around the world.

A patient capital market investor would look for returns that were financially healthy but community focused. Revenues would be recycled back into the community or invested entirely in new mutualist organizations, to begin to anchor a mutualist ecosystem. Small loans would help these new institutions grow, and larger loans would help the ecosystem expand, but lenders would have to remember that the purpose of these loans is to give communities the economic tools to build the institutions they need to help themselves.

Invest in Group Infrastructure

Capital will play another role in building the mutualist future: funding the development of the group infrastructure needed to build new forms of mutualist connection.

What do I mean by "group infrastructure"? When we built the Freelancers Insurance Company, we developed a sophisticated payment-processing system that took in payments from tens of thousands of members and paid that money back out to hundreds of providers. It required a lot of work. Today, there's a payment-processing app that does this automatically: Stripe. Services like Stripe not only take the administrative burden and liability of complex payment processing off companies, but they also put the same technology into the hands of individuals. The barrier to entry to creating an economically linked network around your community has never been lower.

The infrastructure that will support the needs of tomorrow's mutualists is being built today by companies like Google, Slack, Patreon, Kickstarter, Substack, Mobilize, Circle, and Drip, with technologies like distributed ledger technologies such as blockchain. This group infrastructure is enabling people to move out of geographical isolation and come together on new online platforms that make it easier than ever to build an economic infrastructure around a far-flung community—and to do it in a way that both avoids the homogeneity of giant platforms and preserves what's special about the community. We're living through a technological moment that is as important to the shape of our economy's future as the moment when the railroad companies began to lay train tracks across America. Then, America needed physical infrastructure to grow. Today, the most exciting companies are building group infrastructure, which will be the tracks on which we scale the mutualist future.

Because mutualism can and does scale. Just not in the way the for-profit sector can recognize yet. For the mutualist entrepreneur, scale looks like biodiversity, like the long tail, like growth through small enterprises that exist at the local level. If a venture capitalist's goal is to win a market niche, a patient capitalist's goal might be to support as large and diverse a mutualist economic ecosystem as is possible: to fund fifty mutualist organizations in fifty states, for example, each one of which will solve an intractable local social problem.

Solving hard social problems will take longer than building startups. Solving social problems won't have as significant of an upside either, and will require a tremendous amount of work from people who don't mind not getting tremendously rich. The results may not even be visible until the next generation takes the reins, as anyone who has ever planted a young tree knows. And when we succeed, the results won't look like a category-killer like Google. They might, however, solve some of the hardest problems of our time: new models for affordable healthcare; innovative approaches to education, farming, or food access; and the economic pivot to local enterprise needed to address climate change.

But we can't do any of that if we don't see a fundamental change in how we relate to one another. The mutualist future also depends on the future of you.

CHAPTER 10

The Future of You

How to Build

Clumsy your eyes and imagine what a good workday would look like for you.

Where would you be? What would you do? How worried would you be about the notifications on your iPhone? Would you have time to get everything done? Would you have time to take a break to eat or go for a walk? Would you be able to end your workday early to spend time with someone you loved?

The smallest details of our lives are directly related to the economy we live in. But that economy wasn't made by nature. It was made by humans and is the result of very real human decisions, the consequences of which cascade through all of our lives.

Today, many of us are not having a good workday—and we're not having a good workweek or work year. We don't feel secure; we don't have a good plan for retirement; we bear too much of our economic risk on our own. Today's economy—which includes accelerating capitalism, changes in technology that have brought changes in work, and a lack of institutions to address the needs of the new workforce—is leaving us exhausted, exposed, and alone.

Imagine, instead, if technology didn't rob you of your concentration to try to sell you more things, but rather enabled you to build more connection and solidarity with your peers. Imagine if you were an active part of a community organization—or maybe even a part owner of one—that you looked to for benefits, training, and protection from clients who refused to pay you. Imagine if you exchanged skills and services within a whole web of workers and specialists in your community, who bartered and exchanged time with one another.

This is a future we can build. Like the bricklayers who left their marks on buildings erected years ago, we will each be judged in the mutualist future on the basis of how well we've succeeded.

So how can you begin to build? You will find some ideas in the following pages. But for the past decade, we've been trained to be critics. Building begins by changing your orientation away from yourself, away from the critique of government and capitalism, and toward your neighbors regardless of their political stripe or class. Transform those critiques into action. Because when you begin to change your own orientation, you can begin to teach others—activists, workers, elected officials, neighbors, family and friends, foundation leaders, bankers, bakers, and farmers—how to build, too.

Building doesn't need to be complicated. It can be as simple as making yourself a part of a mutualist organization in your own community. But wherever you start, you'll be making a pledge to be a part of the mutualist future and of building tomorrow's safety net—made by workers, for workers. Today, "workers" means all of us.

To find your own entry point into the great vertical of mutualist activity, first ask yourself this basic question: What do I need?

> Look locally for an existing mutualist organization to meet that need. If you can't find a mutualist organization to meet your needs, build one from the ground up.
>
> Go one step further: step up and become a mutualist leader.
>
> If you're a leader in politics or in the foundation world, find a way to support mutualism.
>
> And finally, make yourself a part of mutualist ecosystems—and find ways to protect them.

Ask Yourself: What Do I Need?

Mutualism starts small. Everybody needs to eat: Is there a food co-op near you that you can join? Do you need help with childcare? If so, maybe there's a babysitting cooperative in your community, or maybe you'd like to start one. Is there a local credit union where you can keep your money? What about a community organization: your block association, your local volunteer fire department, a local social justice group, your building's co-op board? It doesn't have to be anything formal. Begin to affiliate yourself with institutions that give you an experience of mutualism. Join the YMCA and attend some classes. Join a quilting club, a running club, a knitting club, a cheese club, a writers club, a soccer league. Maybe there's a local advocacy issue you're passionate about. Show up with an open mind. In short, connect.

When I was a child in Brooklyn Heights, my parents were part of a babysitting cooperative. They used Monopoly money to pay for babysitting, and when they didn't have any left, they would babysit to get more. We all knew one another, and it made me feel so connected to my neighborhood: there were all these parents who loved me and whom I loved in return. This is what mutualism feels like: you start out seeking a solution because you have a need—you don't have the money to spend on traditional childcare—but the by-product is that you might also feel loved.

The key is to follow your instincts and not to worry about the end point for now. Maybe connecting with other people who are in the same boat as you are will lead you to a local church, synagogue, or mosque. Don't worry if it's been a long time since you were part of a religious community, or even if you're skeptical of what you'll find there. The point is that these institutions are cornerstones of communities, and joining one doesn't mean that you have to start believing in God. I know plenty of atheists who participate in religious communities like the Unitarians, the Quakers, or Reform Judaism. These are communities that pride themselves on meeting people where they are. If you live in a small town or city where other opportunities for mutualist connection aren't immediately obvious, consider starting here. Don't discount the power of faith to build community and feelings of connectedness. If you're morally opposed to religion and this doesn't speak to you, that's okay, too.

As you look at your own life and circumstances, assess them truthfully. Don't tell yourself that you occupy too comfortable of a position in society to ask for help. What do you need? How can you ask for help to meet those needs? At the same time, you must also ask yourself what *you* can offer and what kind of future *you're* building. Consider your own needs in the context of the great interconnectivity of all human beings, and make it your top priority to become connected to others, emotionally but also economically.

Once you show up, your second assignment is to have some skin in the game. Be prepared to open your wallet. Charging dues isn't about creating barriers to entry. It's about creating institutions that last. A mutualist organization should be worth whatever amount of money you're putting into it. If money is truly an obstacle, talk to someone. But having skin in the game is part of the point: capital is how mutualist organizations get to do things in the world, how they get to exert real influence. It's how they manage to solve problems, and how they stick around from generation to generation. It's your job to have a stake in that longevity.

Or go one step further. Every organization has leadership positions. Run for one in your organization. When you get elected, ask what more you can do to serve your community better.

If you can't find a mutualist organization in your community, start one yourself. Often, you'll find that other members of the community have been hoping and looking for an opportunity to join together, and you might be surprised to discover that you are exactly the leader they have been waiting for.

Build a Mutualist Organization from the Ground Up

Mutualism doesn't have to start out ambitious, complex, or sophisticated. Consider whether a group you're already part of could benefit by going mutualist. Convene that community and listen to the problems or issues in other members' lives. This is classic organizing. A great resource on this subject is *Rules for Radicals* by Saul Alinsky, but it's easy to find other primers by searching on the Internet for "community organizing," "labor organizing," or any related topic. Start to look for models you can follow or leaders who came before you. Lean on them as resources. Start to have conversations with people you can learn from—but make sure to give something in return. You don't need a lot of money to start, and you don't need new technologies. But you do need to have intention, vision, and leadership.

Maybe you're in a big Facebook group that feels disorganized or a regular meetup, whether virtual or in person, that has few repeat attendees. Maybe you know a small core of devoted members who like being a part of the larger group but would welcome an organization where the commitment is deeper. The easiest way to start a complex mutualist organization is to take an organization that already exists and ask yourself whether a mutualist strategy could benefit it in the long run. Find groups where people already know one another, where there is more trust because of a shared experience, and where problems or challenges that need to be solved are more evident. Elect leaders. Create processes for making decisions. Decide how you will fund your group. This is mutualism at its most basic.

The point is, mutualist organizing doesn't need to be sophisticated or complicated. Starting a block association is as easy as writing a time and a place on a piece of paper and sticking it under your neighbors' doors. Announce you're having a block association meeting at your apartment or house, invite people to come, and make it a potluck. Invite strangers. You'll meet new people, and maybe you'll have an opportunity to help somebody who's alone or who is older and in need. Maybe you'll meet someone who will help you one day when you're in need yourself.

Once you've started your mutualist organization, it's important to remember that the organization is about the members, not about you. It—and you—exist for them, and all of you exist for one another. Invite them into your life and accept the invitation when they do the same. Serve good food. I've been bringing freelancers together for twenty-five years and have learned that this is critical. People are going out on a limb to bring themselves to you; you can reciprocate by providing quality food. It's a metaphor for reciprocity and kindness. When they arrive, listen.

If there isn't a platform to build on, start basic. Use existing tools that help you meet and connect with others. Start your own Facebook group; host a meeting on Meetup; post an event on Eventbrite. Start to let people know you're building an organization and what it's about. Notice who else seems especially interested in what you're doing and give them an assignment to get them more involved. Be clear about your goals and what you intend to do as a group.

Importantly, if you're using a giant platform, keep a separate membership list, even if it's just a spreadsheet. This is the beginning of your database. Eventually, you'll want to lead these people off the platform—remember, you're giving away your data and are beholden to their algorithms—and onto one that gives you more control and autonomy over your organization. In the gold rush of for-profit companies trying to monetize new group infrastructure, it's important to distinguish between technologies with extractive business models and those with business models that are actually built around enabling self-sustaining, independent group activity.

In short, there is a difference between a summation of individuals and a collective of individuals. In a *summation* of individuals, a lot of people come together for a set period of time and for a set project. Kickstarter, GoFundMe, Meetup, CreativeMornings, and Facebook groups are good examples of how technology can be leveraged to create summations. Funding, data, and long-term strategic decisions reside outside the control of participants. There is little sense of mutual obligation, and the tech companies do little to enable real-world human interaction, economic or other, off the platform. Facebook in particular wants to keep people on Facebook. It's a smart company, and if it truly wanted to build independent groups, it would be pushing notifications like "Time to build your member list," "See how your friends are building solidarity?," or "Click here to see how to design a great revenue model!" We call summations of individuals like Facebook groups "communities," but in fact they're just places where individual human activity occurs but never adds up to anything communal. The interaction is solely virtual and is not intended to foster long-term in-person or connected human relationships. These platforms may galvanize individuals quickly, but they don't build lasting collective institutions.

By contrast, a *collective* of individuals enables groups to make decisions that affect everyone. Collectives need active members, leaders, and a process. By definition and design, they are deliberative and slower than summations, and because there may very well be a diversity of opinions, beliefs, and people (from different racial, ethnic, or religious backgrounds), decisions are made with a longer-term view to ensure continuity and relevance. Collectives are harder to build, and fewer of today's technologies for group infrastructure are built around enabling collectivization. Google Groups and Patreon are a start, and new companies like Mighty Networks have the right idea: to enable groups to build their base with a set of tools that allow them to retain their data, member lists, and strategy. Civic Signals is asking how public spaces on the Internet can be leveraged for the public good. I see potential in distributed ledger technology (blockchain) for mutualism because transactions around time and exchange can be recorded to add some formality to what can too often be an ad hoc process (though to my knowledge, no one has built this application yet!).

But at the end of the day, group infrastructure technologies are just tools. Even Google Groups themselves are limited to a few thousand people. Eventually, you'll need to liberate yourself from the technologies that hold you back. I'm sure that the next generation of mutualists will build even better tools using the revenue that they recycle back into their communities.

As your mutualist organization grows, look to the mutualist leaders of the past to remind yourself what mutualism can achieve at scale. The labor and civil rights leaders of the twentieth century were able to change history through the simple power of institutions built on the binding energy of reciprocal obligation. They started small, addressing the most basic needs of their communities. But once they started, they never stopped. They kept building and kept solving problems, until eventually they saw changes that perhaps they never thought could be achieved in their lifetimes.

Become a Mutualist Leader

Regardless of the scale, purpose, or economic mechanism of your mutualist organization, electing a leader, and getting comfortable with the idea of leadership, is a necessity. You might start your mutualist organization by committee, but sooner or later somebody needs to be designated as the adult in the room. A leader needs to be empowered with decision-making authority. The leader must express the will of the organization's members and be answerable to them, but the leader must also be granted a long enough leash to act when tough decisions that don't have a consensus solution need to be made. Without an effective leader, a mutualist organization simply won't be able to get anything done.

For many mutualist groups, one of the most common obstacles to growing into a robust organization is simply getting over the hump of starting to think of itself as an institution that needs to sustain itself and then putting the necessary structures in place to do that. As you start to create these structures, remember the three principles of mutualism: What social problem are you solving, and for what community? What self-sustaining economic mechanism will you use to fund it? How can you build your organization so that it will outlast you when you're gone?

Make a chart: On the right is what you want your organization to look like when it launches. On the left is where you are now.

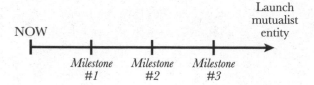

What needs to get done between now and then? Fill in the milestones and then get to work. Bring in a financial person you trust to run the numbers to make sure your organization is sustainable and can at least break even. Bootstrap here. Don't chase crazy ideas until you have a realistic plan for how you can keep the lights on. Professionals may be willing to provide legal, tax, and financial advice for free to help you get started, in hopes of developing an ongoing relationship as your organization grows. You may be able to find foundations and government officials who want to "go mutualist" and will provide seed funding, but don't go looking for outside funding until you have demonstrated that you have an economic there, there. To be clear, that economic mechanism doesn't need to be sophisticated. It can be as simple as the Monopoly money we exchanged in my family's babysitting cooperative, or a time bank in which time itself is the mechanism. Set the ground rules however you like—the point is to have a currency that enables exchange.

Support Mutualism

What if you're a leader in another sector—in government or the charitable foundation world—or you run a successful business, a nonprofit, or a technical assistance company that serves nonprofits? What if you're from a wealthy family and are wondering how best to use your privilege for a social good? What can you do to support mutualism?

Identify an existing group that is addressing a local issue (social justice and equity) or enabling a local activity (providing affordable food or housing) that you want to support. Figure out who the leaders are, invite them in, and ask them what they need to succeed. Listen to what they tell you, and don't assume that you know best: too often nonprofits and charities have opinions about what or whom a local organization should focus on. Your job is to trust these communities and their leaders—and to do no harm. If someone else is already solving the problem you want to solve, partner with them; don't compete with them. Ask them to tell you what they could accomplish in two years if you made an investment in their efforts. Get a strategic plan and look for an economic model that has worked before. Dues, ticket sales, rentals (of equipment or space), selling services, providing technical assistance, and sponsorships are all tried-and-true methods, and though you may find an organization with an innovative economic mechanism, start with economic models that have been proven to work.

Don't ask such organizations to solve every problem at once. Look for strategies and communities that are likely to succeed and start there. Let these organizations build a base of mutualist activity so that they can grow over time to reach a wider swath of the community. Invest only in leaders who are embedded within a group, have a proven record of social entrepreneurship, and have a deep knowledge of their community. You're looking for builders—skilled and intuitive logisticians who have a quest to make order out of chaos.

Or you could start a mutualist capital fund that provides

patient capital to mutualist organizations, similar to the foundation world's program-related investments. The fund could focus broadly, address a specific political issue or geographic region, or even support the local arts—the options are vast.

Most important, your job is not to solve problems for communities that you're not a part of. Your job is to enable those communities to solve their own problems—and to do so however they see fit. Your job is to create institutions that are self-sustaining—independent economic engines that can operate without your input.

Grow Mutualist Ecosystems

As your mutualist organization becomes more sophisticated, look for ways to reach out and connect with other mutualist organizations. Ask for help from them and think about how you can offer something in return. It is this complex network of reciprocal obligation that allows mutualist organizations to thrive and eventually to knit themselves together into the kind of mutualist ecosystems that undergird major social change.

In 2005, a journalist named Dan Buettner wrote an article for *National Geographic* titled "The Secrets of a Long Life." Buettner had discovered a handful of regions around the world—Okinawa in Japan, Sardinia in Italy, Nicoya in Costa Rica, Icaria in Greece, and Loma Linda in California—where people appeared to be living statistically longer, healthier lives. He called these regions "Blue Zones" and wrote a *New York Times* bestseller detailing what made them special. One commonality he found among them was a high level of social engagement in spiritual, family, and civic life. In Blue Zones, people avoid isolation and loneliness, and they have lower levels of depression. I call these places mutualist ecosystems: communities that have invested in the kind of institutions that make us feel human. If we're healthier and live longer, that's great. But what is important is that we live well, and that we live humanely while we do.

How can we build mutualist ecosystems in every city, so that this kind of civic engagement doesn't exist just in wealthy, progressive neighborhoods? I think we already are doing this. Even before the COVID-19 pandemic began to change the economics and demographics of cities, the dominance of mega urban centers like New York and San Francisco had started to give way to secondary cities like Durham, North Carolina, and Pittsburgh, Pennsylvania, and by 2020 tertiary cities—places like Kingston, New York; Newark, New Jersey; and Albuquerque, New Mexico—were also on the rise. Cooperatives such as Co-op Cincy, Co-op Dayton, and the Evergreen Cooperatives in Ohio or Cooperation Jackson in Mississippi are sprouting up all across the United States, and I expect that in time, new towns and cities will become new centers of mutualist activity as well.

Mutualist ecosystems are precious. They're like UNESCO World Heritage sites: equal parts powerful and fragile. If you find them, listen to their leaders, support them, and then get out of the way. Help them stay independent and let them flourish.

Imagine the end of your ideal workday. You are meeting up with friends to eat good, affordable food. During the meal, you talk about change: the change you want to build for yourself and the change you want to build for your community.

That conversation—about change, about what a safety net that meets your real needs as a worker looks like—is the same conversation that workers have been having for hundreds of years. It's how the great mutualist leaders of the past, those who succeeded in linking workers together—across political lines, race, sexuality, gender, and generations—got started. Today, new leaders are stepping into the field: a generation that understands that the way we've drawn political boundaries has nothing to do with workers' real needs. This generation, I hope, will be able to see that workers who have turned to one another—like the garment workers of the 1910s, the autoworkers of the 1930s, the civil rights organizers of the 1960s, the rural cooperative grocers of the 2010s, and the urban mutual aid organizers of 2020—are all doing the same thing: helping themselves, and one another, by taking responsibility for their own destinies. When we turn to one another, we find that we already have the collective wisdom and grit to build our shared security—a new social contract—once again.

You don't need to be a mutualist leader to get meaningfully involved in the mutualist future. People will come to mutualism from many different perspectives, experiences, expertise, and political ideologies. And that's okay. In fact, it's the point. Mutualism is how communities all over the world have met their most basic needs for hundreds of years. And it's how we'll meet our own needs tomorrow.

But there is so much work still to be done. Creating mutualist ecosystems isn't easy and won't happen overnight. It takes face-to-face contact and courage. It takes a desire to solve problems and to build. It takes a willingness to focus on what you share with others, not on what divides you.

After all, it's the builders who change the world. Now go be one of them.

When New York City shut down in March of 2020, my family and I moved our work, religious, and social lives into our home. So many of the routines that brought me into contact with the communities that make me who I am—work, faith, social—were disrupted. As businesses shuttered, as we left our work spaces for our homes, and as everyone I knew settled into the new normal of isolation, I did something I'd never done before: I attended a religious service virtually.

Instead of sitting in the Brooklyn Heights Synagogue, my husband and I found ourselves in front of a laptop in our living room, livestreaming a Friday night Shabbat service. Alone at the bimah in the center of the sanctuary where we used to gather as a community stood our rabbi, Serge Lippe, dressed in his tallit as usual. Socially distanced even from the piano player because of the pandemic, he had nonetheless assembled us virtually. Our congregation was scattered: some were alone, others were sheltering in groups. And yet we were also here together, just as we would have been on any other Friday night.

Our community was intact. I realized we were going to be okay.

In the coming weeks, our synagogue's leadership made sure that every person in our congregation heard from someone else and felt the warmth of our community, wherever they were. I asked if I could help make phone calls. I'm glad

I did. I could feel the gratitude that the people I called felt for our synagogue. It was the kind of gratitude I'd seen only in times of celebration or despair. It was as though our institution was a living organism, capable of holding all of its congregants in a reassuring and hopeful embrace.

I am still moved by the image of our rabbi alone at the bimah, ministering to his flock. But what moved me most wasn't the power of the rabbi. It was *our* power—our power as a community that was still intact, in spite of everything. That power was built on every time we'd been together in the past: every time we'd celebrated a simcha or a bar or bat mitzvah, and every time we'd visited another member's home after a death. It was built on every High Holy Day, and on the hours and hours we'd spent together, year after year. That power reassured us that we were not alone in the world, that we were connected, and that each of us made up a part of our congregation's whole.

We were a community. And during those dark hours, we held ourselves together.

Acknowledgments

To Sarah Burnes, my agent: you made this book happen. You saw the book's potential when it was just a kernel of an idea, and your patience and support never flagged. You began as my agent; you are now my friend. And you are a friend to the mutualist movement.

To Mark Warren, my editor at Random House: thank you for insisting that the book "meet the moment" and for showing me how I could make that happen. You delivered your wisdom through "screaming notes" and during our many discussions (in your wonderful Texas drawl), and I will always be grateful for it. You also marshaled a wonderful team at Random House that included Joseph Perez, who produced the exquisite book cover; Craig Adams, who took such great care with the copy; and Chayenne Skeete, who provided guidance along the way.

To Andy Kifer: Thank you for your much appreciated contribution to the writing of this book. Your organizational talents were indispensable, especially when it came to wrangling my complicated ideas and making them a reality on the page. Also, thank you for working with Hilary McClennan and Julia Knoerr to make sure that the fact-checking was so thorough.

For their keen insights and thoughts that made this book so much better: Many thanks to Professor Jessica Gordon Nembhard, Michael Peck, Matt Hancock, and Professor Sharryn Kasmir.

So much of what's in this book came out of my experience with the Freelancers Union. A big, heartfelt thank-you to the directors, staff, and members of that organization, past, present, and future. (During production of the book, I was delighted to get a note from member Barb Jatkola, one of Random House's crack team of freelance copy editors.)

For Ann Boger, whom I have worked with to build the freelancers mutualist ecosystem for the last fourteen years: You are a joy to work with, decent to your core, and definitely the smartest person in the room.

Let me particularly express my gratitude to Trisala Chandaria and Hanan Kolko, who joined the Freelancers Union board early on and stayed to pass the baton to the next generation. Thanks also to board members, freelancers, and staff, Ohad Folman, Dina Sena, Julie Lamb, Diallo Powell, Caitlin Pearce, Randy Liu, Rick Koven, Judy Osteller, Mark Snyder, Richard Winsten, and Monica Alexandris-Miller, who all made remarkable contributions to building the organization and keeping it going.

Thanks, too, to the extraordinary insights of Charles Heckscher, whose book *New Unionism* was one of my guides in the early years, and whose thoughts on New Mutualism were essential to my vision for the Freelancers Union.

The Freelancers Union would never have been possible

without years of support and patient capital from the Ford Foundation. Many thanks also to the MacArthur Foundation and to the Rockefeller Foundation. Janice Nittoli at Rockefeller understood early on the importance of freelancers in our new economy and was instrumental in creating the Freelancers Insurance Company. Also, I never would have even begun this journey without the support of Echoing Green and of my dear friend Cheryl Dorsey.

Actuaries never get the thanks they deserve—except here. Thanks to the fearless actuaries Mike Sturm, Jeffrey Shue, and Dan Skwire for their devotion to helping freelance workers get the insurance they need in this new economy. I love you guys!

I have created several organizations and businesses for freelancers—some worked out; some didn't. But I will forever appreciate the investors who understood that their support was about the mission and whose integrity and kindness shone through when times were hard. I'm thinking particularly of Alfred Lin of Sequoia, Tim Collins and team of Ripplewood Advisors, Ommeed Sathe and Miljana Vujosevic from Prudential's Impact and Responsible Investment Unit, Chris Murumets from RGAx, and Andrea Hippeau at LH.

I want to especially acknowledge Bill Drayton of the Ashoka Foundation, and the many years of friendship and wonderful mentoring I've received from him. Bill's long career has been a model for how to make your life in service to something greater than yourself. I look forward to many more years of collaborating with him.

Many thanks also, for their guidance and friendship, to Greg Scholl, Adria Goodson, Andy Golden, Jon Gertner, Professor Michael Mushlin, Andrea Phillips, and Kyle Zimmer.

To the late Cornell ILR Professor Clete Daniel for your classes on labor history: You taught me to look to the past for examples of how workers can build organizations to better their lives, even in the face of a greed-driven and chaotic world.

Special thanks to Leyla Vural for sharing her academic work on the mutualist ecosystem built in the early twentieth century by the Amalgamated Clothing Workers of America. Also to Walter Naegle, life partner of the great late Bayard Rustin, for giving me insight into how Bayard helped bring the spirit of India's nonviolent liberation movement to the American civil rights struggle.

On a more personal note, I want to acknowledge my fore-bears: Sara Horowitz the first, who came to America and became the matriarch and anchor of the Horowitz family. Her six girls and two boys went on to form the Horowitz Cousins Club, a mutualist institution if there ever was one. I never met my grandfather Israel Horowitz, but he taught me so much by example. I live by his favorite phrase for bursting the bubble of pretension: "Excuse me, but I am allergic to bullshit."

My sister, Anne, has been tethering me to the universe for many decades now, and I am eternally grateful to her. Her judgment is spot-on and impeccable. That includes her deci-sion to marry Ron Sexton, and to have their daughter, Nata-lie Sexton.

To Michele Molotsky, my best friend since our first DSA meeting.

And to my annual January 13th friends, who have made it a mutualist gathering—our economic mechanism is wine! I love you all!

Thanks to Dorothy Day!

To my husband, Peter DeChiara, whom I have known since high school: I still find your integrity and wit compelling. Thanks for being just the right person for me after all these years.

Finally, thank you to two women who have given my life more joy and meaning than I can express: my mother, Bernice Horowitz, who taught me how to be in the world with fortitude and a strong point of view, and my wonderful daughter, Rachel Horowitz, who has turned out to be just the kind of smart, funny, and strong woman my mother would have loved.

Notes

One: "Horowitz Says We Shall Make No More Brassieres"

21 Israel Horowitz was only thirteen: "Israel Horowitz, Union Leader, Dies: Was Vice President of the I.L.G.W.U.," *New York Times,* October 15, 1957.

22 Israel was a member of the Local 25: Ibid.

22 The ILGWU's membership ballooned: "Timeline," the Kheel Center ILGWU Collection, Cornell University ILR School, https://ilgwu.ilr.cornell.edu/timeline/index.html.

22 "HOROWITZ SAYS": While this story is famous in my family, I've never been able to find the actual newspaper clipping.

22 As he moved up: "Israel Horowitz, Union Leader, Dies."

23 Eventually, Israel became: Ibid.

23 $40 billion in assets: "Investments with Impact," Amalgamated Bank, https://www.amalgamatedbank.com/institutional-investing.

29 "a new deal for the American people": Franklin D. Roosevelt, "Acceptance Speech to the 1932 Democratic Convention," July 2, 1932, Franklin D. Roosevelt Presidential Library and Mu-

seum,https://www.fdrlibrary.org/documents/356632/390886/
1932+DNC+Acceptance+Speech.pdf/.

30   more than a third: Gerald Mayer, "Union Membership Trends
in the United States" (CRS Report for Congress, August 31,
2004), 22–23, https://digitalcommons.ilr.cornell.edu/cgi/view
content.cgi?article=1176&context=key_workplace. Comparisons
between historical union membership rates are necessarily ap-
ples to oranges since public sector workers could not unionize
until the 1960s. In 1954, 35 percent of workers who were eligible to unionize were unionized, but the total workforce was only
28 percent unionized. The question of how to measure union
density in America persists to this day.

32   representing 7.5 percent: Ibid.

35   Thomas Frank gives: Thomas Frank, *Listen, Liberal, or What Ever
Happened to the Party of the People?* (New York: Picador, 2016), 46.

36   "The country had merely exchanged": Ibid., 79.

36   "The left and right each drifted": Paul Collier, *The Future of
Capitalism: Facing the New Anxieties* (New York: Harper, 2018), 9.

37   "The U.S. labor movement has never recovered": Charles J.
Whalen, "Echoes of a Broken Strike," *Washington Post*, August 5,
2006.

38   From 1955 to 2019: U.S. Bureau of Labor Statistics, "Union
Members Summary," news release, January 22, 2020, https://
www.bls.gov/news.release/union2.nr0.htm.

42   Even in 2018, 57 million: Freelancers Union and Upwork,
"Freelancing in America 2018: 5th Annual Report," https://
assets.freelancersunion.org/media/documents/freelancingin
americareport-2018.pdf.

42   In July of 2020: Sheryl Gay Stolberg, "Millions Have Lost Private Health Insurance in Pandemic-Driven Recession," *New
York Times*, July 13, 2020.

42   By 2027, a majority of Americans: Freelancers Union and
Upwork, "Freelancing in America: 2017," https://assets.free
lancersunion.org/media/documents/FreelancingInAmerica
Report-2017.pdf.

Two: Early Mutualism

47   most plant species: B. Wang and Y.-L. Qiu, "Phylogenetic Distribution and Evolution of Mycorrhizas in Land Plants," *Mycorrhiza* 16, no. 5 (2006): 299–363, https://doi.org/10.1007/s00572-005-0033-6.

47   one single-celled blob: E. G. Leigh, Jr., "The Evolution of Mutualism," *Journal of Evolutionary Biology* 23, no. 12 (December 2010): 2507–2528, https://doi.org/10.1111/j.1420-9101.2010.02114.x.

47   As Yuval Noah Harari writes: Yuval Noah Harari, *Sapiens: A Brief History of Humankind* (New York: Harper Perennial, 2018), 40–50.

48   the "commoning" instinct: David Bollier and Silke Helfrich, eds., *Patterns of Commoning* (Amherst, Mass.: Commons Strategies Group, 2015), 1.

48   A plaque in the Rochdale Pioneers Museum: Amanda Keddie and Martin Mills, *Autonomy, Accountability and Social Justice: Stories of English Schooling* (New York: Routledge, 2019), 75.

48   first self-identified anarchist: John Bucci, "Searching for the Meaning of Anarchism," *Journal of Education* 154, no. 2 (1971): 61–68, https://doi.org/10.1177/002205747115400210.

48   The two thinkers were: Robert Hoffman, "Marx and Proudhon: A Reappraisal of Their Relationship," *Historian* 29, no. 3 (1967): 409–430, https://doi.org/10.1111/j.1540-6563.1967.tb01785.x.

49   "ourselves the leaders of a new intolerance": Pierre-Joseph Proudhon to Karl Marx, May 17, 1846, Correspondence of Pierre-Joseph Proudhon, Marxists.org, accessed August 19, 2020, https://www.marxists.org/reference/subject/economics/proudhon/letters/46_05_17.htm.

50   "Mutualism operates, by its very nature": Quoted in James J. Martin, *Men Against the State: The Expositors of Individualist Anarchism, 1827–1908* (Colorado Springs: Ralph Myles, 1970), 133.

50   "leaders of a new intolerance": Proudhon to Marx, May 17, 1846.

50   "The Jew is the enemy": Quoted in William I. Brustein and Lou-
      isa Roberts, *The Socialism of Fools?: Leftist Origins of Modern Anti-
      Semitism* (New York: Cambridge University Press, 2015), 35.

51   If, as Russell Shorto argues: Russell Shorto, *Amsterdam: A History
      of the World's Most Liberal City* (London: Abacus, 2014), 18.

52   "Early humans, in their migratory roaming": Ibid., 30.

52   "Once the peat loses its water": Ibid., 30–31.

53   "Residents banded together": Ibid., 48.

53   Citizens started to pay taxes: Herman Havekes et al., "Water
      Governance: The Dutch Water Authority Model" (Dutch Water
      Authorities, The Hague, 2017), https://dutchwaterauthorities
      .com/wp-content/uploads/2019/02/The-Dutch-water
      -authority-model-2017.pdf.

53   Eight centuries later: Ibid.

53   Hence the Dutch maxim: Shorto, *Amsterdam*, 48–49.

55   "In America I encountered": Alexis de Tocqueville, *Democracy in
      America*, ed. and trans. Harvey C. Mansfield and Delba Win-
      throp (Chicago: University of Chicago Press, 2000), 489–492.

56   "Everywhere that, at the head": Ibid.

56   We can trace the origins: "About Us," Philadelphia Contribu-
      tionship, https://1752.com/blog/about-us/history/.

56   arose out of another association: John Thomas Scharf and
      Thompson Westcott, *History of Philadelphia, 1609–1884* (Phila-
      delphia: L. H. Everts, 1884), 2114.

57   members contributed equally to a fund: "About Us," Philadel-
      phia Contributionship.

57   143 such policies: "Insurance Ben-efactor," Citizen Ben, PBS,
      https://www.pbs.org/benfranklin/l3_citizen_insurance.html.

57   It is from Franklin's: John Bainbridge, *Biography of an Idea: The
      Story of Mutual Fire and Casualty Insurance* (Garden City, N.Y.:
      Doubleday, 1952), 50–54.

57   "free Africans and their descendants": William Douglass, *Annals
      of the First African Church* (Philadelphia: King & Baird, 1862), 15,
      http://name.umdl.umich.edu/agv8875.0001.001.

58   "We . . . do unanimously agree": Ibid., 16.

59   Officially organized in 1787: Charles Nordhoff, *The Communistic Societies of the United States* (1875; repr. New York: Dover, 1966), 117–256.

59   We owe the hymn "Simple Gifts": "Simple Gifts," Alfred Shaker Museum, https://www.alfredshakermuseum.com/history/simple-gifts/.

59   A Shaker community: Nordhoff, *The Communistic Societies of the United States*, 117–256.

60   "the largest and most successful communal experiment": Nicholas C. Vincent, "Shaker Furniture," Heilbrunn Timeline of Art History, Metropolitan Museum of Art, https://www.met museum.org/toah/hd/shak/hd_shak.htm.

61   Other Utopian societies included: Nordhoff, *The Communistic Societies of the United States*, 117–256.

61   A journalist named Charles Nordhoff: Ibid., 386.

61   That would be close to $280 million: The U.S. Bureau of Labor Statistics looks back only to 1913, so I've relied on Measuring-Worth (https://www.measuringworth.com/), an Illinois non-profit, for this estimate.

61   "enjoyed a greater amount of comfort": Nordhoff, *The Communistic Societies of the United States*, 386–406.

64   "Social capital," he writes: Robert Putnam, *Bowling Alone: The Collapse and Revival of American Community* (New York: Touchstone, 2001), 19.

64   Putnam sees social capital: Ibid., 92.

65   Ten million Americans are: "Introduction to Multiemployer Plans," Pension Benefit Guaranty Corporation, https://www.pbgc.gov/prac/multiemployer/introduction-to-multiemployer-plans.

65    $197 billion: U.S. Department of Agriculture, "Agricultural Cooperative Statistics 2017" (USDA Rural Development Service Report 81, December 2018), https://www.rd.usda.gov/files/publications/SR81_CooperativeStatistics2018.pdf.

Three: Mutualist Organization

69   In his discussion of social capital: Robert Putnam, *Bowling Alone: The Collapse and Revival of American Community* (New York: Touchstone, 2001), 22.

71   Food co-ops: FAQ, Park Slope Food Coop, https://www.food coop.com/faq/.

72   often attributed to the Great Law of Peace: According to one source, this attribution may be apocryphal, but it serves nonetheless to illustrate a useful point. Peter Wood, "Seventh Generation Sustainability—A New Myth?," National Association of Scholars, https://www.nas.org/blogs/article/seventh _generation_sustainability_-_a_new_myth.

77   A 2016 study: Brian J. Grim and Melissa E. Grim, "The Socioeconomic Contribution of Religion to American Society: An Empirical Analysis," *Interdisciplinary Journal of Research on Religion* 12 (2016), article 3, http://www.religjournal.com/pdf/ ijrr12003.pdf.

78   18.5 percent of all hospitals: F. A. Curlin, "On the Opinions of US Adults Regarding Religiously Affiliated Health Care Facilities," *JAMA Network Open* 2, no. 12 (2019): e1919013, https:// doi.org/10.1001/jamanetworkopen.2019.19013.

79   in 2017 the biggest: "Global 500 for 2019," International Cooperative and Mutual Insurance Federation, https://www .icmif.org/publications/global-500/global-500-2019.

80   "In a lending circle": Sophie Quinton and National Journal, "The Immigrant Lending Circles That Pave the Way to Citizenship," *Atlantic*, July 8, 2013.

81   $197 billion, with about $93 billion: U.S. Department of Agriculture, "Agricultural Cooperative Statistics 2017" (USDA Rural Development Service Report 81, December 2018), https://www.rd.usda.gov/files/publications/SR81_Cooperative Statistics2018.pdf.

81   three million cooperatives: "Facts and Figures," International Co-operative Alliance, https://www.ica.coop/en/cooperatives/ facts-and-figures.

81   the ground floor of 31 Toad Lane: "Our Story: Rochdale Pioneers Museum" (brochure, Co-operative Heritage Trust, Manchester, UK, n.d.), http://australia2012coop.com/downloads/Coop_Museum_brochure_v12.pdf.

82   voluntary and open membership: "Cooperative Identity, Values & Principles," International Co-operative Alliance, https://www.ica.coop/en/cooperatives/cooperative-identity?_ga=2.219880282.253173022.1597868358-600095709.1596723450.

83   fourteen million Americans: "Union Members—2019," U.S. Bureau of Labor Statistics, news release, January 22, 2020, https://www.bls.gov/news.release/pdf/union2.pdf.

Four: Mutualist Ecosystems

87   Detroit, Michigan, declared bankruptcy: Monica Davey and Mary Williams Walsh, "Billions in Debt, Detroit Tumbles into Insolvency," *New York Times,* July 18, 2013.

87   Puerto Rico followed suit: Mary Williams Walsh, "Puerto Rico Declares a Form of Bankruptcy," *New York Times,* May 3, 2017.

87   Hartford, Connecticut, has been on the brink: Rick Rojas and Mary Williams Walsh, "Hartford, with Its Finances in Disarray, Veers Toward Bankruptcy," *New York Times,* August 15, 2017.

89   The Amalgamated Clothing Workers of America was founded: Steven Fraser, *Labor Will Rule: Sidney Hillman and the Rise of American Labor* (Ithaca, N.Y.: Cornell University Press, 1993), 88–91.

89   Under Hillman, the Amalgamated: Ibid., 114–115.

89   Hillman realized he needed patient capital: Jacob S. Potofsky, "The Pioneering of Workers' Banks," *AFL-CIO American Federationist,* May 1963.

90   Amalgamated Bank of New York opened its doors: Ibid.

90   The bank made no loans: Jacob S. Potofsky, "Trade Unions Enter Business," in *New Tactics in Social Conflict,* ed. Harry W. Laidler and Norman Thomas (New York: Vanguard Press, 1926), 47.

90   Amalgamated Bank hired experts: Potofsky, "The Pioneering of Workers' Banks."

90   limiting the ownership of stocks and dividends: Potofsky, "Trade Unions Enter Business," 51.

90   "In the case of the labor bank": Ibid.

91   By 1926, the list of businesses: Ibid., 39–40.

91   At its height: Fraser, *Labor Will Rule*, 213.

91   By 1927, Hillman was building: Leyla F. Vural, "Unionism as a Way of Life" (PhD diss., Rutgers University, 1994), 206.

92   Ground was broken: Ibid., 216.

92   The new buildings were managed: Ibid., 217.

92   Once the buildings were built: Ibid., 222.

93   the first Sidney Hillman Health Clinic: "A Union Health Center Expands," *Social Service Review* 26, no. 1 (1952): 89–90, www .jstor.org/stable/30021373.

93   The clinic operated at its original: "The Institute's Sidney Hillman/Phillips Family Practice Is Relocating to Two Brand New Locations in December," Institute for Family Health, news release, November 7, 2017, https://institute.org/news/ relocating-union-square-location/.

99   Ten days in, I read a column: Bob Herbert, "In America; Workers, Unite!," *New York Times*, September 14, 1994.

100   Bob Herbert wrote a great piece: Bob Herbert, "In America: Strength in Numbers," *New York Times*, November 3, 1995.

102   "a pioneer in shaping institutions": "Sara Horowitz, Attorney and Workers' Rights Leader, Class of 1999," MacArthur Foundation, https://www.macfound.org/fellows/611/.

105   Founded in 1956: Rebecca Henderson and Michael Norris, "1worker1vote: MONDRAGON in the U.S." (Harvard Business School Case 315-103, February 2015; rev. September 18, 2015), 3.

105   "They say that necessity": Michael Peck, interview with author and Andy Kifer, March 2, 2020.

106   He set up a technical school: Henderson and Norris, "1worker-1vote," 3–4.

106   "He found his life's mission": Peck interview.

106 In 1959, Arizmendi convinced: Henderson and Norris, "1worker1vote," 4.

107 more than eight times: "Ten Union Co-op/Mondragon Principles," 1worker1vote, Michael Peck, email correspondence from Michael Peck to author, March 6, 2020.

107 The technical school: Ibid.

107 70 percent of its profits: Henderson and Norris, "1worker-1vote," 5.

107 $13.5 billion in revenue: Ibid., 1.

107 "If the Basque region": Josu Ugarte, "What's Next for the World's Largest Federation of Worker-Owned Co-ops?," interview by Mary Hansen, *Yes!*, June 12, 2015, https://www.yesmagazine .org/economy/2015/06/12/world-s-largest-federation-of -worker-owned-co-operatives-mondragon-josu-ugarte/.

107 In the aftermath of the financial crisis: Henderson and Norris, "1worker1vote," 8.

107 "Fagor had a forty-to-forty-five-year run": Peck interview.

108 Rather than lay off: Henderson and Norris, "1worker1vote," 8.

108 "His North Star": Peck interview.

108 "Mondragon depends on": Ibid.

109 "There's an incredible commercial movement": Ibid.

109 In a region of only 4 million people: Figures on numbers of cooperatives in the region vary widely from source to source, but most cite somewhere between 7,500 and 15,000. These statistics are from: John Restakis, "The Emilian Model—Profile of a Co-operative Economy," http://library.uniteddiversity.coop/ Cooperatives/Emilia_Romagna/The_Emilian_Model -Profile_of_a_Co-operative_Economy.pdf.

109 The result is that Emilia-Romagna: Tito Menzani and Vera Zamagni, "Cooperative Networks in the Italian Economy," *Enterprise & Society* 11 no. 1 (March 2010), 108–118, https://www .jstor.org/stable/23701221?seq=1.

110 "The people who came back from the hills": Matt Hancock, interview with author and Andy Kifer, April 20, 2020.

111 "recognized the interest of the nation": Menzani and Zamagni, "Cooperative Networks in the Italian Economy," 105.

111 New laws over the following decades: Ibid., 104–107.

115 "chaordic structure": For more on chaordic structure, see Dee Hock, *Birth of the Chaordic Age* (Oakland, Calif.: Berrett-Koehler, 2000).

Five: Mutualist Transformation

119 Instead, the cover shows two men: *Life*, September 6, 1963, cover, Library of Congress, https://www.loc.gov/exhibits/brown/brown-aftermath.html#obj217.

121 one of the very first Black mutual aid societies: Often thought to be the first Black mutual aid society in America, the Free African Society was actually the second, according to Professor Jessica Gordon Nembhard of John Jay College. The first was established in Newport, Rhode Island, in 1780. Jessica Gordon Nembhard, *Collective Courage: A History of African American Cooperative Economic Thought and Practice* (University Park: Pennsylvania State University Press, 2014), 42.

121 Absalom Jones and Richard Allen: Dennis C. Dickerson, "Our History," African Methodist Episcopal Church, https://www.ame-church.com/our-church/our-history/.

121 It took some time: Ibid.

122 By 1856, it had expanded: Clarence E. Walker, "The A.M.E. Church and Reconstruction," *Negro History Bulletin* 48, no. 1 (1985): 10, https://www.jstor.org/stable/44176613.

122 That same year, the church started Wilberforce University: "About Wilberforce University," Wilberforce University, https://wilberforce.edu/about-wilberforce/.

122 the church took public stands: Walker, "The A.M.E. Church and Reconstruction," 10–12.

122 Randolph's father was one minister: Manning Marable, "A. Philip Randolph and the Foundations of Black American Socialism," in *Workers' Struggles, Past and Present: A "Radical America" Reader*, ed. James Green and Paul Buhle (Philadelphia: Temple

University Press, 1983), 214, https://www.jstor.org/stable/j
.ctv6mtdnm.16.

123 "In every period of American history": Gordon Nembhard,
Collective Courage, 28.

123 "A group of people who know each other": Ibid., 42.

124 Black schools: Ibid., 34.

124 insurance companies: Ibid., 61.

124 credit associations and banks: Ibid., 62.

124 a Black cooperative shipyard: Ibid., 63.

124 There were Black cooperative associations: Ibid., 55.

124 "provide the economic opportunities": Ibid., 15.

124 "high-level social and economic cooperation": Ibid., 33.

125 the Knights of Labor took a wide view: Elizabeth Faue, *Rethinking the American Labor Movement* (United Kingdom: Taylor & Francis, 2017), 20–21.

125 as many as 60,000 Black members: Robin D. G. Kelley, "Building Bridges: The Challenge of Organized Labor in Communities of Color," *New Labor Forum*, no. 5 (1999): 47, https://www
.jstor.org/stable/40314314.

126 a Jewish immigrant from London: "Samuel Gompers," AFL-CIO, https://aflcio.org/about/history/labor-history-people/
samuel-gompers.

126 "business unionism": Bernard Mandel, "Gompers and Business Unionism, 1873–90," *Business History Review* 28, no. 3 (1954): 264–275, https://www.jstor.org/stable/3111574.

126 especially against the Chinese: Gompers wrote racist things like "The Yellow Man finds it natural to lie, cheat, and murder." Quoted in Arthur Mann, "Gompers and the Irony of Racism," *Antioch Review* 13, no. 2 (1953): 209, https://doi.org/10.2307/
4609631.

126 "What does labor want?": "What Does Labor Want?" (paper presented to International Labor Congress, Chicago, September 1893), Sam Gompers Papers, University of Maryland, http://www.gompers.umd.edu/More.htm.

127   In 1925, a group of Pullman porters: Marable, "A. Philip Randolph," 220.

127   Some historians credit the porters: Larry Tye, "Pullman Porters Helped Build Black Middle Class," interview with Steve Inskeep, NPR, May 7, 2009, https://www.npr.org/transcripts/103880184.

127   Randolph fought the Pullman Company: Arthur C. McWatt, "'A Greater Victory': The Brotherhood of Sleeping Car Porters in St. Paul," *Minnesota History* 55, no. 5 (1997): 207, https://www.jstor.org/stable/20188023.

128   "a machine for the propagation": Marable, "A. Philip Randolph," 221.

128   Randolph's efforts as the head: McWatt, "'A Greater Victory,'" 209.

128   In 1928, his application to the AFL: Marable, "A. Philip Randolph," 221.

128   After years of dogged organizing: McWatt, "'A Greater Victory,'" 212.

128   By 1941, the specter: Marable, "A. Philip Randolph," 223–224.

129   Bayard Rustin was born: Rob Lukens, "History's People: Remembering Bayard Rustin," Chester County Historical Society, February 23, 2012, http://www.chestercohistorical.org/historys-people-remembering-bayard-rustin.

129   Randolph issued these demands: "June 1941," Franklin D. Roosevelt Day by Day, The Pare Lorentz Center at the FDR Presidential Library, http://www.fdrlibrary.marist.edu/daybyday/resource/june-1941-9/.

129   But Rustin, who had poured: Scott H. Bennett, *Radical Pacifism: The War Resisters League and Gandhian Nonviolence in America, 1915–1963* (Syracuse, N.Y.: Syracuse University Press, 2003), 122.

130   He worked on behalf: Ellie Rushing, "Pa. Civil Rights Icon Bayard Rustin Gets Posthumous Pardon," *Philadelphia Inquirer,* February 6, 2020.

130   he was arrested in Tennessee: Bayard Rustin, *I Must Resist: Ba-*

yard Rustin's Life in Letters (San Francisco: City Lights Books, 2012), 22.

130   in 1947, he organized the Journey: "Freedom Rides," Britannica .com, https://www.britannica.com/event/Freedom-Rides.

130   in 1953 he was arrested: Bayard Rustin, *I Must Resist,* 149.

130   "it was an absolute necessity": Bayard Rustin, quoted in Michel Martin, "In Newly Found Audio, a Forgotten Civil Rights Leader Says Coming Out 'Was an Absolute Necessity,'" *All Things Considered,* NPR, January 6, 2019. The audio is from an interview with Rustin published in *The Washington Blade* in the mid-1980s.

131   "I think it's fair to say": "Bayard Rustin—Who Is This Man?," *State of the Re:Union,* n.d., https://web.archive.org/ web/20130516061236/http://stateofthereunion.com/home/ season-2/bayard-rustin#.

131   "As I was ushered in": Cynthia Taylor, *A. Philip Randolph: The Religious Journey of an African American Labor Leader* (New York: New York University Press, 2006), 184.

131   By early 1961: "The Places of Bayard Rustin," National Park Service,   https://www.nps.gov/articles/the-places-of-bayard-rustin .htm.

132   the executive director . . . (Randolph himself): "Organizing Manual No. 2: Final Plans for the March on Washington for Jobs and Freedom," booklet, New York, n.d., 3, https://www .crmvet.org/docs/moworg2.pdf.

132   "*Organizational* sponsorship": Ibid., 6.

133   "We planned out precisely the number of toilets": Henry Louis Gates, Jr., "Who Designed the March on Washington?," PBS, https://www.pbs.org/wnet/african-americans-many-rivers-to -cross/history/100-amazing-facts/who-designed-the-march -on-washington/.

133   "We urge all marchers": "Organizing Manual No. 2," 10.

134   "comprehensive and effective *civil rights legislation*": Ibid., 4.

Six: What Does Labor Want?

140 59 percent of independent contractors: Freelancers Union and Upwork, "Freelancing in America 2019," Results Deck, https://www.upwork.com/i/freelancing-in-america/.

140 Growing up in Canarsie: Jessica Bruder, "Driven to Despair," *New York*, May 14, 2018, available at Intelligencer, https://nymag.com/intelligencer/2018/05/the-tragic-end-to-a-black-car-drivers-campaign-against-uber.html.

141 "I was the most skilled": Douglas Schifter, "To Those It May Concern," Facebook, February 5, 2018, https://www.facebook.com/permalink.php?story_fbid=1888367364808997&id=100009072541151.

141 Eventually, in 2004: Bruder, "Driven to Despair."

141 "Unable to spare the time": Ibid.

141 It was around this time: Alyson Shontell, "All Hail the Uber Man! How Sharp-Elbowed Salesman Travis Kalanick Became Silicon Valley's Newest Star," *Business Insider,* January 11, 2014.

142 "Everywhere he looked": Bruder, "Driven to Despair."

143 "Forget about a great country": Schifter, "To Those It May Concern."

143 "Police responded, taping off the scene": Bruder, "Driven to Despair."

145 only 10.3 percent: U.S. Bureau of Labor Statistics, "Union Members Summary," news release, January 22, 2020, https://www.bls.gov/news.release/union2.nr0.htm.

147 It was Saturday, March 25, 1911: Steven Greenhouse, *Beaten Down, Worked Up: The Past, Present, and Future of American Labor* (New York: Knopf, 2019), 60–79.

147 One man kissed a woman: Henry Lee, "Triangle Shirtwaist Factory Fire: How One of NYC's Worst Disasters Improved Workers' Rights," New York *Daily News,* August 14, 2017.

147 "They would hit the sidewalk": Frances Perkins, "Remembering: The 1911 Triangle Factory Fire" (lecture, Cornell Univer-

sity School of Industrial and Labor Relations, September 30, 1964), https://trianglefire.ilr.cornell.edu/primary/lectures/.

147 One hundred and forty-six: Greenhouse, *Beaten Down, Worked Up*, 65.

147 She worked alongside: Ibid., 70.

147 "in New York I could": Ibid., 71.

147 "the day the New Deal was born": Ibid., 67.

149 Greenhouse tracks Frances Perkins's rise: Ibid., 71–72.

149 Roosevelt won the election: Ibid., 72–73.

149 Perkins had a sweeping vision: Ibid., 73.

150 "I see no reason why": Ibid., 77.

150 Union membership increased from 7.5 percent: Gerald Mayer, "Union Membership Trends in the United States" (CRS Report for Congress, August 31, 2004), 22–23, https://digitalcommons.ilr.cornell.edu/cgi/viewcontent.cgi?article=1176&context=key_workplace.

151 "A better relationship between labor": Franklin D. Roosevelt, "Franklin Roosevelt's Statement on the National Labor Relations Act (The Wagner Act)," July 5, 1935, Franklin D. Roosevelt Presidential Library and Museum, http://docs.fdrlibrary.marist.edu/odnlrast.html.

152 In a short section: "The National Labor Relations Act," The National Labor Relations Board, https://www.nlrb.gov/guidance/key-reference-materials/national-labor-relations-act.

153 workers began to drop: "Flint Sit Down Strike (1936–37)—UAW History," documentary video, UAW Public Relations Department, 2012, posted to YouTube, https://www.youtube.com/watch?v=mZ7v1FQJTiQ.

153 But by late 1936: Sidney Fine, *Sit-Down: The General Motors Strike of 1936–1937* (Ann Arbor: University of Michigan Press, 1969), 156.

154 Two years later, Walter Reuther: Nelson Lichtenstein, *Walter Reuther: The Most Dangerous Man in Detroit* (Urbana: University of Illinois Press, 1995), 135–136.

154   "represented one of the industrial union movement's": Ibid., 140.

155   "earned so little": A. H. Raskin, "A Union with 'Soul,'" *New York Times*, March 22, 1970.

155   Mount Sinai, Beth Israel: "A Look Back: 1199's 46 Days That Turned New York Upside Down," 1199SEIU, May 7, 2014, https://www.1199seiu.org/nycli/a_look_back_1199_s_46 _days_that_turned_new_york_upside_down-1.

156   "Van Arsdale couldn't have worked harder": Raskin, "A Union with 'Soul.'"

157   "The unionization of finance": Nelson Lichtenstein, *State of the Union: A Century of American Labor* (Princeton, N.J.: Princeton University Press, 2002), 120.

158   Taft-Hartley also introduced: Robert J. Rosenthal, "Exclusions of Employees Under the Taft-Hartley Act," *Industrial and Labor Relations Review* 4, no. 4 (1951): 556–570, https://doi.org/10 .2307/2518498.

158   "There is no 'magic' or set number": "Independent Contractor (Self-Employed) or Employee?," IRS, https://www.irs.gov/ businesses/small-businesses-self-employed/independent -contractor-self-employed-or-employee.

160   On April 16, 2020: I calculated these numbers using Google Finance's historical stocks data, comparing pandemic lows to where these indexes were on April 16, https://www.google .com/finance/.

161   The very same day: Nelson D. Schwartz, "'Nowhere to Hide' as Unemployment Permeates the Economy," *New York Times*, April 16, 2020.

161   You've probably seen graphs like this one: Christopher Ingraham, "U.S. Stocks Continue to Post Big Gains. But What About Wages?" *Washington Post*, January 14, 2020.

162   "Forming a union is a great tool": Bryan Menegus, "Leaked Memo Shows Kickstarter Senior Staffers Are Pushing Back Against Colleagues' Union Efforts," Gizmodo, March 21, 2019.

Seven: The Future of Labor

167 *The president wants you to join the union!:* "John L. Lewis," AFL-CIO, accessed August 21, 2020, https://aflcio.org/about/history/labor-history-people/john-lewis.

168 currently represents 21,000: "New York Taxi Workers Alliance Mission & History," New York City Taxi Workers Alliance, http://www.nytwa.org/mission-and-history.

168 "From the beginning, we've always": Mischa Gaus, "Taxi Workers Become a Union—Officially," Labor Notes, October 20, 2011, https://labornotes.org/blogs/2011/10/taxi-workers -become-union%E2%80%94officially.

169 started in 2018 on the heels: Emily Witt, "L.A. Drivers Strike Against Uber and Lyft," *New Yorker,* May 9, 2019.

169 "What is a reasonable commission": Noam Scheiber and Kate Conger, "Uber and Lyft Drivers Gain Labor Clout, with Help from an App," *New York Times,* September 20, 2019.

170 a number of large-scale strikes: Witt, "L.A. Drivers Strike Against Uber and Lyft."

170 protested at California governor Gavin Newsom's office: Juliana Feliciano Reyes, "The Philly Connection to the Uber and Lyft Drivers' Strike in L.A.," *Philadelphia Inquirer,* March 25, 2019.

170 articulated a "Drivers Bill of Rights": "Drivers Bill of Rights," Rideshare Drivers United, accessed August 21, 2020, https://drivers-united.org/p/drivers-bill-of-rights.

171 Consider Study Hall: At my insurance startup Trupo, I partnered with Study Hall, which helped get the word out about our freelancer-focused insurance to its members. To learn more about Study Hall, go to https://studyhall.xyz/.

172 more than 31,000 members: Caty Enders, "Binders Full of Women Writers: Can a Secret Facebook Group Be Inclusive?," *Guardian,* August 5, 2015.

174 "Drivers' work is outside": Andrew J. Hawkins, "Uber Argues Its Drivers Aren't Core to Its Business, Won't Reclassify Them as Employees," The Verge, September 11, 2019.

174   More than half of all freelancers: Freelancers Union and Up-
       work, "Freelancing in America 2018: 5th Annual Report,"
       https://assets.freelancersunion.org/media/documents/free
       lancinginamericareport-2018.pdf.

177   Critics hold that the Independent Drivers Guild: Noam
       Scheiber, "Uber Has a Union of Sorts, but Faces Doubts on Its
       Autonomy," *New York Times*, May 12, 2017.

178   Company unions started in the 1920s: "About," Communica-
       tions Workers of America, https://cwa-union.org/about/cwa
       -history.

178   700,000 members: Ibid.

178   supported Democratic candidate Bernie Sanders's: "CWA En-
       dorses Sen. Bernie Sanders for President," Communications
       Workers of America, press release, December 17, 2015, https://
       cwa-union.org/news/entry/cwa_endorses_sen_bernie_sanders
       _for_president.

178   "The blue-collar blues": Studs Terkel, *Working: People Talk About
       What They Do All Day and How They Feel About What They Do*
       (1974; repr. New York: Ballantine, 1989), xiv.

Eight: The Future of Government

182   "People around here haven't spent": Jack Healy, "Farm Coun-
       try Feeds America. But Just Try Buying Groceries There," *New
       York Times*, November 5, 2019.

184   Today, New York State alone has more than eighty: "New York
       State CDFIs," New York State CDFI Coalition, accessed Octo-
       ber 1, 2020, https://www.nyscdfi.org/nyscdfis.

187   revenues of more than $2 trillion today: Brice S. McKeever,
       "The Nonprofit Sector in Brief 2018: Public Charities,
       Giving, and Volunteering," Urban Institute, National Center
       for Charitable Statistics, November 2018, https://nccs.urban
       .org/publication/nonprofit-sector-brief-2018#the-nonprofit
       -sector-in-brief-2018-public-charites-giving-and-volunteering.

190   "If you get hit by an asteroid": Ommeed Sathe, interview with
       author and Andy Kifer, May 22, 2020.

191   130,000 union members: "About the Culinary Health Fund," Culinary Health Fund, https://www.culinaryhealthfund.org/about-us/.

Nine: The Future of Capital

196   "At a very high level": Ommeed Sathe, interview with author and Andy Kifer, May 22, 2020.

197    $40 billion in assets: "Investments with Impact," Amalgamated Bank, https://www.amalgamatedbank.com/institutional-investing.

198   restricting members' ability to resell: Leyla F. Vural, "Unionism as a Way of Life" (PhD diss., Rutgers University, 1994), 218.

198   Ace Hardware, which was founded in 1924: Clare O'Connor, "How Ace Hardware Turned Corner Stores into a $4.7 Billion Co-op," *Forbes,* March 5, 2015.

198   Land O'Lakes, which dates back to 1921: "Farmer Owned Since 1921," Land O'Lakes, https://www.landolakesinc.com/What-We-Do.

198   Green Bay Packers: "2020 Annual Meeting of Shareholders," Green Bay Packers, https://www.packers.com/community/shareholders.

199   Roanoke Electric Cooperative: "Our History," Roanoke Electric Cooperative, https://www.roanokeelectric.com/about-us/our-history/.

200   "Profits are merely the yardstick": Jacob S. Potofsky, "Trade Unions Enter Business," in *New Tactics in Social Conflict,* ed. Harry W. Laidler and Norman Thomas (New York: Vanguard Press, 1926), 51.

203   "In 1983, I founded Grameen Bank": Muhammad Yunus, "Sacrificing Microcredit for Megaprofits," *New York Times,* January 14, 2011.

Ten: The Future of You

220   Okinawa in Japan, Sardinia: Dan Buettner, *The Blue Zones: Lessons for Living Longer from the People Who've Lived the Longest* (Washington, D.C.: National Geographic, 2008).

Index

Sara Horowitz is a practicing mutualist. The daughter of a labor lawyer and the granddaughter of a former vice president of the International Ladies' Garment Workers' Union, she is the recipient of a MacArthur Foundation "genius grant" and the Eugene V. Debs Award for her pioneering work supporting the needs of part-time, independent, and freelance workers.

In 1995 she founded Working Today, the nonprofit that became the Freelancers Union. For over twenty-five years, the Freelancers Union has been an anchor of a mutualist ecosystem that built a political coalition around working freelancers, who are left out of most labor legislation and are the vanguard of today's changing economy. The Freelancers Union created the Freelancers Insurance Company, a portable benefits solution for independent workers; created Spark, a mutualist network of local resources for freelancers all over the country; and led the successful "Freelance Isn't Free" campaign in New York City, resulting in landmark legislation preventing wage theft for independent workers. It continues its advocacy work on behalf of freelancers to this day.

Horowitz is the founder and CEO of Trupo, a Sequoia Capital–backed insurance startup for independent workers, and has served as the chair of the Board of the Federal Reserve Bank of New York. She has been featured in *The New York Times*, *The Wall Street Journal*, *The Economist*, *Wired*, *The Atlantic*, and *Fast Company*, and on National Public Radio's *Talk of the Nation* and *All Things Considered*. Her first book, *The Freelancer's Bible* (Workman, 2012), was named one of *Forbes*'s "Best Books to Boost Your Career." She has been recognized as one of the World Economic Forum's 100 Global Leaders for Tomorrow and was selected as one of Politico's "Politico 50" in 2015. Horowitz is a lifelong resident of Brooklyn, New York, where she lives with her family.